MW01078638

Changing
Our Mind

A call from America's leading evangelical
ethics scholar for full acceptance
of LGBT Christians in the Church

Second Edition

February 2015

David P. Gushee

Read The Spirit Books

an imprint of
David Crumm Media, LLC
Canton, Michigan

To find out about David Gushee's talks and appearances, visit

www.ChangingOurMind.org

Copyright © 2015 by David P. Gushee

All Rights Reserved New Revised Standard Version Bible, copyright 1989, Division of Christian Education of the National Council of the Churches of Christ in the United States of America. Used by permission. All rights reserved.

ISBN: 978-1-939880-93-2

2nd Edition, with 2014 Reformation Project Speech

Cover art and design by
Rick Nease
www.RickNeaseArt.com

Published By
Read The Spirit Books
an imprint of
David Crumm Media, LLC
42015 Ford Rd., Suite 234
Canton, Michigan, USA

For information about customized editions, bulk purchases or permissions, contact David Crumm Media, LLC at info@ DavidCrummMedia.com

Contents

*In honor of LGBT Christians who still love
a church that has not loved them.*

Acknowledgments

THE 17 ESSAYS collected in the main body of this book were published in similar form by Baptist News Global (BNG)—formerly ABPnews/Herald—from July to October 2014. BNG is an autonomous, nonprofit news organization that offers news, features and opinion articles every business day for an international audience of Baptists and other Christians. The author and publisher gratefully acknowledge the quite gracious permission granted by BNG for the rapid publication of these opinion pieces into this book. BNG has gone above and beyond the call of duty in this regard. To see the original pieces, and the dialogue they created as each was published, go to www.baptistnews.com.

I am grateful to a handful of friends who read this manuscript in its development stage, and for all who dialogued with my original articles online. Your comments have contributed to substantial improvements. Of course, responsibility for the content of this manuscript falls entirely on its author.

This second edition contains minor corrections, edits, and updates, with one exception—at the request especially of LGBT Christian leaders, I have included the full text of my speech at the Reformation Project conference in Washington, D.C. in November 2014.

All scripture is quoted in the New Revised Standard Version except where otherwise noted.

Books by David P. Gushee

Evangelical Social Ethics: Converting America and Its Christians, 1944-2014 (*Library of Theological Ethics*). With Isaac B. Sharp. Louisville: Westminster John Knox Press, forthcoming 2015.

In the Fray: Contesting Christian Public Ethics, 1994-2013. Eugene, OR: Cascade Books, 2014.

Evangelical Peacemakers: Gospel Engagement in a War-Torn World. Eugene, OR: Cascade Books, 2013.

"Glen Harold Stassen: Baptist Peacemaker, Global Christian Ethicist" (*Festschrift*), Co-Editor/Contributor, with Reggie L. Williams. *Perspectives in Religious Studies*. Vol. 40, no. 2 (Summer 2013).

The Sacredness of Life: Why an Ancient Biblical Vision is Key to the World's Future. Grand Rapids: William B. Eerdmans Publishing Company, 2013.

Yours is the Day, Lord, Yours is the Night, with Jeanie Gushee. Nashville: Thomas Nelson, 2012.

A New Evangelical Manifesto: A Kingdom Vision for the Common Good. St. Louis: Chalice Press, 2012.

Religious Faith, Torture, and Our National Soul. With Jillian Hickman Zimmer and J. Drew Zimmer. Macon: Mercer, 2010.

The Scholarly Vocation and the Baptist Academy. With Roger Ward. Macon: Mercer, 2008.

The Future of Faith in American Politics: The Public Witness of the Evangelical Center. Waco, TX: Baylor, 2008.

Only Human: Christian Reflections on the Journey toward Wholeness. San Francisco: Jossey-Bass, 2005.

Getting Marriage Right: Realistic Counsel for Saving and Strengthening Marriages. Grand Rapids: Baker, 2004.

Kingdom Ethics: Following Jesus in Contemporary Context, with Glen H. Stassen. Downers Grove, IL: Intervarsity, 2003. Translations current and forthcoming: Japanese, Bulgarian, Spanish, Indonesian, Chinese, Korean, Arabic, Finnish. Excerpt anthologized in *Living Ethics,* edited by Michael Minch and Christine Weigel. Belmont, CA: Wadsworth, 2009.

Christians and Politics Beyond the Culture Wars: From Despair to Mission. Grand Rapids: Baker, 2000.

Toward a Just and Caring Society: Christian Responses to Poverty in America. Grand Rapids: Baker, 1999.

The Future of Christian Higher Education. Co-Editor and Contributor, with David S. Dockery. Broadman & Holman, 1999.

A Bolder Pulpit: Reclaiming the Moral Dimension of Preaching, with Robert H. Long. Valley Forge: Judson Press, 1998.

Preparing for Christian Ministry: An Evangelical Approach. With Walter Jackson. Grand Rapids: Baker, 1996.

*The Righteous Gentiles of the Holocaust: A Christian
    Interpretation*. Minneapolis: Augsburg Fortress
    Press, 1994. German Translation: *Die Gerechten Des
    Holocaust: Warum nur wenige Christen den Juden halfen*.
    Wuppertal: One Way Verlag, 1997. Second Edition:
    *Righteous Gentiles of the Holocaust: Genocide and Moral
    Obligation*. St. Paul, MN: Paragon House, 2003.

Praise For
Changing Our Mind

"This book is courageous, clear, balanced, and like everything David Gushee writes, deeply grounded in biblical faith. He takes theology and the Bible with utter seriousness, continuing in his role as a leading evangelical scholar around questions of ethics and discipleship. David's description of how his mind has changed on LGBT issues will be a challenge to some, an inspiration to others, but a gift to all who find themselves at some point on this journey."

Wesley Granberg-Michaelson served as General Secretary of the Reformed Church in America from 1994 to 2011. He was one of the first managing editors of Sojourners magazine and plays an active role in ecumenical organizations.

"In this landmark volume, renowned evangelical ethicist David Gushee issues a passionate call for biblically minded Christians to re-think their traditional opposition to same-gender relationships. Gushee presents clear and compelling scriptural arguments for understanding marriage as a faithful, lifelong covenant that is available to gay and straight couples alike. This book will be seen as a major milestone in evangelical engagement with LGBT issues. A must-read for Christians seeking a compassionate, biblically faithful response to the same-sex marriage controversy."

Mark Achtemeier, theologian, scholar and author of The Bible's Yes to Same-Sex Marriage: An Evangelical's Change of Heart.

∽

"David Gushee is one of the most thoughtful evangelical theologians writing today. I have known David for quite some time and have been moved to witness how his heart and his mind have changed on LGBT inclusion and Christianity. His is not a story of instant transformation, but of many years and long hours listening, praying and continually returning to Biblical study for guidance. Like Jacob wresting with the Angel, David has wrestled to understand God's calling for Christians at this moment when they struggle mightily to understand how to be true to their faith and to their LGBT sisters and brothers, daughters and sons, mothers and fathers. Far from asking us to park our beliefs at the church door, David forges a path to liberation. By admitting that the Church got it wrong about the LGBT community, he shows us how we can embrace a more authentic, more responsible, more loving and finally truer faith. I have been longing for just this book for many years and I can't recommend it more highly."

Sharon Groves served as director of the Religion and Faith Program at the Human Rights Campaign. She developed training tools and resources to help families welcome LGBT family and friends from a faith perspective.

∽

"David Gushee's book is a rare glimpse into the process of deep paradigm-shifting by an extremely thoughtful and accomplished Christian ethicist. It lays out the moral, ethical, and biblical questions surrounding the LGBT controversy clearly and comprehensively. Moreover, Gushee helpfully clears away a host of false stereotypes on both sides of the debate, making distinctions that will help the whole church focus more clearly on core issues as it struggles through this paradigm-changing question. Gushee addresses one of the most controverted issues in our time, and does so with wisdom and grace."

James V. Brownson is an educator, theologian, New Testament scholar and the author of Bible, Gender, Sexuality: Reframing the Church's Debate on Same-Sex Relationships.

~

"Progress scares many people—especially when it moves quickly and feels uncontrollable. David P. Gushee's new book will help people feel more comfortable with an issue they have been in deeper and deeper conflict over as progress on understanding gay, lesbian, bisexual and transgender people continues. When I first read his earlier book, 'Righteous Gentiles of the Holocaust,' I realized immediately how a complicated subject had been brought so much better into focus. The book allowed for significant change in my own life. I came to understand that religious teachings too often play the most significant role in creating a climate of hostility toward innocent and vulnerable LGBT people—especially youth. I know from personal experience that a book like 'Changing Our Mind' will save lives and minds."

Mitchell Gold is co-founder of a furniture and home furnishings company with stores across North America. He is the author of Crisis: 40 Stories Revealing the Personal, Social, and Religious Pain and Trauma of Growing Up Gay in America. In 2005, Gold founded www.FaithInAmerica.org to counter the harm caused to LGBT men and women by exclusionary religious teachings.

"Thank you David Gushee for the courage to share so beautifully and articulately what God has shown you. 'Changing our Mind' is a must-read for anyone who struggles with how sexual orientation fits together with a life of faith. Praise God for patiently guiding each of us to this place of new understanding, as God moves the Church into the 21st century."

Jane Clementi co-founded The Tyler Clementi Foundation with her husband Joseph after their son Tyler committed suicide as a result of a Rutgers University cyberbullying incident. The foundation promotes education, research and public programs to promote inclusive communities for LGBT youth.

⁓

"Evangelical scholar David Gushee reads scripture in a way that is deeply pleasing to those of us in the rabbinic tradition who believe that scripture is the spoken Word of God delivered to instruct us on how to live in His image every day. [With my whole heart I seek you; let me not wander from your commandments! I have stored up your word in my heart, that I might not sin against you. Psalm 119:10-11] David Gushee honors the authority of the Word, as we do. [Open my eyes, that I may behold wondrous things out of your law. Psalm 119:18] Like us, he would not dare act on his own first impressions or interpretations of the Word. Like us, he subjects his mind and heart first to the disciplines of careful text study: carefully reading through the long history of readings by the sages who preceded him, carefully examining the context in which his community of believers reads the Word today, and carefully attending to the immediate reason why he is reading now and with whom and for whom. [So Ezra the priest brought the Law before the assembly, both men and women and all who could understand what they heard, on the first day of the seventh month. ... And Ezra opened the book in the sight of all the people, for he was above all the people, and as he opened it all the people stood. And Ezra blessed the Lord ... the Levites, helped the people to understand the Law, while the people remained in their places. They read from the book, from the Law of God, clearly, and they gave the sense, so that the people understood the reading.]

"By way of his obedient, humble and learned reading of scripture in the context of his Christian community's daily life in this American context and this time, evangelical ethicist David Gushee brings the living and loving letter of the Word to his gay brothers and sisters as he for so many years has brought it to all his fellow believers in the Church and in the Synagogue as well. That this is a man of God is evident to us who live outside his church as well as to those who live within it, to all of us who hope in God's redemptive presence.

"I confess that I care about Christian religious and theological work when I believe it glorifies the God of Israel and serves the Word of love and instruction, justice and mercy that I hear in the Torah. This is a Word that demands uncompromising service to the One who alone created all the world and the creatures in it. And this is a service that includes uncompromising care for God's creatures ... For all these reasons I care deeply about the religious and theological and caring work of Rev. David Gushee. I honor him as a servant of the creator and of the Word that demands care for God's creatures. I have witnessed such service in the way he teaches and preaches, reads and interprets scripture; and in the way he listens to the heartbeats, praises, words and cries of people around him, within his church community and outside it, and in the way he listens to the God who listens to them, each and all. All this is present, once again, in his most recent book, *Changing Our Mind*. Here he narrates how his heart, mind, spirit and judgment changed about the place of LGBT Christians in the Church ... It is a remarkable book from many perspectives. *Spiritually*: to witness this ingenuous narrative from a many-leveled religious, intellectual, and spiritual leader, confessing and apologizing for those years, during which he sincerely understood his evangelical Christianity and his obedient reading of scripture to preclude his accepting LGBT Christians in the Church. *Following the heart-filled intellect*: to follow the point by point clarity of this man's reasoning, from how and why he failed to accept, to each of the slowly growing sincerely developing individual steps of experiencing, observing, studying, praying and thinking that led him to the conclusion announced by this book: that it is time now for him — and those who share his devotion to scripture and to all members of the church — to honor those LGBT Christians who come to sit with him and them in the pews. Scripturally: to see such close and deep reading of the many verses of scripture pertinent to these themes, to see what it means for no word or verse to be ignored, no spirit- and mind-filled scholarship to be ignored, and no implication of reading to be ignored so that, in the fullness of this moment of reflection in the fullness of embodied life in the church, these profound questions of our age could be addressed without loss of faith and loss of compassion."

Peter Ochs is the Edgar Bronfman Professor of Judaic Studies at the University of Virginia.

Foreword

IF YOU DON'T know who David Gushee is, you should.

If I were to say he's the Billy Graham or Pope Francis of American evangelical ethics, you'll say, "Then why don't I know about him already?" The answer would be that, just as there are reasons few people think of English cuisine or Northern hospitality, there are reasons people don't immediately associate deep, philosophical and ethical reflection with evangelical theology.

But just as there are great English chefs, and just as there are truly hospitable people up north, there are great evangelical ethicists. And for decades now, David Gushee has earned the reputation as America's leading evangelical ethicist.

In this book, he admits that he has been wrong on the LGBT issue. He explains why he has changed his mind and heart. Like a good math student, he "shows his work."

It's not every day that a religious leader makes a confession like this.

Older readers will remember when Billy Graham shocked American evangelicals—first, by refusing to segregate his evangelistic events, and then, by working with Roman

Catholics. Younger readers will remember when Pope Francis shocked Catholics by washing the feet of a Muslim woman, or by refusing to condemn gay Catholics.

You're about to read something like that in these pages, but maybe even more startling and unexpected.

Not only is David Gushee's work deep, thoughtful and brilliant; and not only is David philosophically and theologically careful and astute; he is also refreshingly clear and understandable by "common people" who know neither philosophical nor theological mumbo jumbo.

He follows the ethic of Jesus by letting his yes be yes and his no be no.

David aims for yes-no clarity in these pages—and brevity as well. No other writer I know of has handled the famous so-called "clobber passages" with clarity and brevity equal to David's.

There's one more thing I must say before closing. I respect and admire David greatly, and I sincerely and genuinely like him. And I should admit that I feel a good bit of pain for him as I anticipate this book being published.

Like him, I used to tacitly follow the party line. Like him, I went through a slow process of rethinking. Like him, my thought process was enriched and intensified by family members and friends who came out to me, along with members of the church I pastored. Like him, I have many regrets for people I hurt and for advice and opinions I gave that I now wish I could take back.

When I "came out" as a married heterosexual evangelical pastor who had changed my mind on LGBT equality, I received hate mail that I still wince to remember. Friendships ended. Major evangelical magazines put me on their black list. I found that there are theological bullies in the evangelical world who don't mind throwing their weight around. Speaking invitations and friendly welcomes dried up in places where I had formerly felt welcome and at home.

These experiences hurt. And along with my own discomfort, I felt hurt for the friends who found themselves forced to choose between friendship with me and belonging to their churches, denominations or associations. I realized that by going public with my own change of mind and heart, I was putting many of my friends in a difficult position. I didn't like doing that.

And now I know that David is facing all these realities. He is too good of a human being and Christian gentleman to have to experience these things. But then again, he is too good of a human being and Christian gentleman to hide his change of mind and heart in order to avoid experiencing these things.

Which leads me to a warning: If you have the courage to read these pages and take to heart what this ethicist presents, you will face a big ethical decision of your own. If you change your mind, if you experience a change of heart on this issue, you, too, will face some consequences, to which you will have to respond—ethically. That process could well be a defining moment in your own ethical development. And of course, chickening out—being unwilling to honestly and seriously engage with David's clear and heartfelt thinking in these pages—will be a kind of ethical defining moment as well.

Funny, isn't it? Just when we want to focus on the ethical splinter in the eyes of those who see the LGBT issue differently (from whichever side), we may just have to face the ethical logs in our own.

—Brian D. McLaren

Brian D. McLaren is a best-selling author who has written more than a dozen books about building bridges across the chasms that can separate religious, cultural and political groups. He also is a frequent guest on television, radio and news media programs, talking about the challenge of peacemaking in a turbulent world.

Preface

BACK IN THE days of my wine and roses when I was a young college instructor, one of the staples of the Freshman English syllabus was a unit on Discourse. A considerable block of class time spent on Discourse in a required foundational course might seem a bit antique to us now; but back then it made all kinds of practical sense. Beyond that and truth told, I reveled in teaching it.

For one thing, teaching the wonders of Discourse trumped, hands down, a number of other parts of those earlier Freshman English syllabi. Beyond that, however, there is an art and a kind of austere beauty that are singular to Discourse as a division of literature, primarily because, as a modus operandi, Discourse demands a clarity of thought and an integrity of argument that do not always accrue in other forms of written or spoken communication; and of all the forms and presentations of Discourse, the *apologia* is the most beautiful.

Apologia is not, of course, a word we use very often nowadays, and most certainly not in everyday conversation. Yet we all have some awareness of it. For instance, *Socrates' Apologia Pro Vita Sua (An Apology for His Life)*, is one of the great classics of Western literature and, quite literally, has affected every one of us in one way or another, whether we realize it or not. More to the point, however, whether we give a piece of work its formal name or not, we all recognize and almost instantly respect the "Apology" or *apologia*, when we are fortunate enough to chance upon it.

Apologia is that form of Discourse that, while sharing all the required characteristics of clarity and integrity, goes beyond them. It, in a manner of speaking, humanizes them. The creator of an *apologia* dares to speak personally ... autobiographically and candidly and always vulnerably ... about his or her engagement with the ideas and progress of ideas being presented. The result, for the reader or hearer, is not only an intimacy of engagement with ideas cogently and clearly presented, but also a kind of awe in the face of an overwhelming humility by the speaker of the Apology. The result, in sum, then, and in other words, is a thing of rare luminousness and docile beauty. The Apology is what it is—a story, if you will, of a man or woman wrestling an idea with complete nakedness in the face of the grandeur of that idea.

Changing Our Mind is an *apologia*. It is an *apologia* by one of the most respected and highly credentialed conservative religion scholars and thinkers of our times. Enter it with anticipation, certainly, but also with gratitude—gratitude that a man of such stature as David Gushee has paid us, as his readers, the ultimate compliment. He has chosen to recount publicly and in detail, his wrestling with and his conclusions about the theological issues separating many traditional Christians from embracing the full inclusion into the body of Christ of their fellow Christians who are members of the LGBT family. Such words as these are fashioned only with wrenching effort on the part of their author. They are, as I have said, *apologia* at its best.

   —*Phyllis Tickle*

Phyllis Tickle is a scholar of religion, a journalist, an author of 36 books and is widely regarded as a leading American expert on religious publishing. An active member of the Episcopal church, she speaks widely at universities and professional conferences and often is interviewed in prominent news media, including TIME magazine, the New York Times, USA Today, PBS, CNN and the BBC.

Introduction

CHRISTIANITY IN THE West faces a crisis of moral authority.

This crisis is evident in the hemorrhaging of members of my own generation—Millennials—from church pews.

It is evident in the church's waning influence in public policy debates, and in the lack of Christian leaders who command the same cultural clout that C.S. Lewis and Billy Graham once did.

There are many reasons for this crisis, of course, from the church's ill-fated embrace of partisan politics to its widespread apathy regarding racial and economic injustice.

But no single issue has been more consequential in separating my peers from the church—and making them doubt the moral credibility of their leaders—than the evangelical church's ongoing rejection and exclusion of LGBT people.

Many established Christian leaders do not have close relationships with gay, lesbian, bisexual or transgender Christians, so they are more likely to view the "LGBT issue" through a political lens rather than a relational one. Given the controversy surrounding the issue, they generally choose to accept the status quo in order to focus on matters that seem less fraught with peril.

Meanwhile, the young people in their congregations don't have the luxury of avoiding the challenging questions this issue raises. Our best friends from church tearfully tell us they are gay and have anguished over that fact for years. Our peers at school come out and don't feel safe to set foot in a church again. For Millennial Christians, this issue isn't an abstract political football. It's a question of how much space and grace we will make for friends we dearly love, and friends whose differences have made them feel incredibly alone, afraid and unloved.

So when we look to many of our church leaders and see unbudging opposition or fear in the face of controversy, we begin to realize that we will have to go elsewhere for answers. As our friends are shown the door, we watch as our pastors decline to open their hearts, privileging their careers and reputations over meaningful engagement with the tears and trials of many we love the most. Our leaders continue to preach about the self-sacrificing love of Jesus, but their words ring more and more hollow in light of their actions.

The consequences here aren't hard to predict: Millennials are leaving the church. Critically, they aren't leaving because the cost of discipleship is too high, but because the number of leaders willing to suffer that cost is too few.

Despite that sobering reality, most established evangelical leaders remain stuck in their ways, or at best, simply at a loss for how to move forward. Many older, more conservative church members threaten to pull their support from anyone who shifts their thinking, preventing pastors and others from seriously grappling with this issue. That dynamic repels many of our most promising young people. The result: The church is losing one of its best hopes for a thriving future—and the very change-agents who could help to reverse these downward trends. Understandably, this situation leaves many pessimistic about the place of the church in the 21st century.

Into this scene enters David Gushee, a brave and generous man who is uniquely positioned to help the church overcome this crippling crisis. A prolific writer and thinker, David Gushee has amassed sterling theological credentials in the wing of the church where this crisis is most acute: evangelicalism. With the leading evangelical ethics textbook (*Kingdom Ethics*) among the 19 books to his name, Gushee carries wide influence among many evangelical leaders, pastors and scholars.

Importantly, Gushee has not been afraid to take unpopular, countercultural stances in the past. When many American Christians wavered on the moral acceptability of torture, Gushee stood firm in denouncing the practice, drafting the "Evangelical Declaration Against Torture." Likewise, he took the lead in drafting the "Evangelical Climate Initiative," challenging those who would turn our stewardship of God's creation into a partisan political issue.

In *Changing Our Mind*, Gushee again puts his reputation on the line to defend an unpopular position among his peers: That the church must apologize for the harm it has inflicted on the LGBT community, and that our interpretation of Scripture on same-sex relationships has been at the root of that harm.

Some will no doubt assume that, in taking this stand, Gushee is simply caving in to the changing cultural landscape of America. But that is precisely the opposite of what this book represents. Just as he did on torture and creation care, Gushee is cutting directly against the grain of the broader evangelical culture. He is acting out of conviction rather than expediency, for it should go without saying that—at least in the near-term future—he has far more to lose than to gain by aligning himself with LGBT Christians.

But just as importantly, Gushee is also challenging the views of many of those who already support same-sex relationships. Although it often isn't acknowledged in more progressive circles, Christians who are uneasy about same-sex marriage are not without legitimate concerns. Their concerns about compromising the authority of Scripture and watering down the church's sexual standards are not unfounded, nor are they eased by pro-LGBT arguments that can essentially be whittled down to "Paul was a man of his times" and "love is love."

David Gushee, to his great credit, does not dismiss or trivialize those concerns. Instead, he issues a clarion call to LGBT-affirming Christians to honor the full authority of the Bible. He also makes a bold, compelling case for affirming the church's historic teaching that sex is for marriage—not simply for consenting adults, and not simply for expressing love as defined by feelings. By addressing the core concerns of conservative Christians with respect and reasoned argument, Gushee points the way forward beyond the church's present impasse.

David Gushee's work in this book stands to be of pivotal importance in reframing the LGBT dialogue in the church, and in reclaiming the church's moral authority for a new generation. One day, even many of those who respond with dismissal and outrage now will thank him for it. Certainly, I and other LGBT Christians already have much reason to be grateful.

—Matthew Vines

Matthew Vines is the founder of the Reformation Project, a Bible-based, nonprofit organization that seeks to reform church teaching on sexual orientation and gender identity. Matthew took a leave from his studies at Harvard University to research what the Bible says about homosexuality. As a result, he produced the best-selling book, God and the Gay Christian: The Biblical Case in Support of Same-Sex Relationships. He has appeared in news stories nationwide, including in the pages of USA Today, the Washington Post and the New York Times. He lives in Kansas.

CHAPTER 1

Live From New York

MAYBE IT WAS predictable that my struggle over "the LGBT issue" would finally become unbearable in New York City, where the gay rights movement started.[1]

I was in "The Big Apple" in 2013 for one of those off-the-record invitation-only confabs that make people feel really important. The host was one of America's hottest young evangelical (theologically conservative Protestant Christian) leaders. This talented young man had invited about a dozen mainly 20- and 30-something evangelical up-and-comers (and a few oldsters like me, recently having reached the shocking age of 50) to come to a conference room in Manhattan for a one-day meeting to talk together about our work and dreams.

I remember almost nothing of what was said at the meeting—other than the numerous offhand comments along

---

1 Language matters, and terminology related to this issue is both shifting and contested. I have chosen to use the term LGBT throughout this book to refer to lesbian, gay, bisexual and transgender people, and their relationship to the Church, as my main subject. A longer list is sometimes employed, such as LGBTQIA, but that seemed unwieldy to me.

the way about the LGBT issue and its relation to evangelical
Christianity.

This is not at all uncommon. You can't turn around these
days in Christian circles without bumping into the gay issue. It
has become the hottest of all hot potatoes in evangelical Christianity, as it has in much of U.S. and global culture. It has a
particular twist these days among young, hip and often urban
evangelicals. Such evangelicals, with their skinny jeans and
café macchiatos, under no circumstances want to be like or to
sound like their oh-so-square evangelical forebears of the previous generation. They do not want to sound hateful, they do
not want to be demagogues, and they do not want to be confused with Christian Rightists like ye olde Jerry Falwell. And
they really want to share the Gospel effectively in big, sophisticated urban centers like New York.

Such young evangelical movers and shakers are caught
between two very powerful forces in their own religious sub-
culture. On the one hand, older leaders in their world still
hold extraordinary power to open or close doors to younger
evangelicals who are climbing their career ladders in the religion business. These older leaders are almost unanimously
closed to any reconsideration of this issue, and so far they
have the power to exclude anyone who might even want to
open that conversation. For many evangelicals, this makes
fresh thinking literally unthinkable.

On the other hand, well-informed 30-something evangelicals are plenty aware of dissent bubbling up from their
younger coreligionists. They know that the "evangelical consensus" is not fully persuading the youth group kids and
Christian college students who populate our grassroots. Many
of these kids have made clear to pollsters and anyone else who
is listening that they find the traditional Christian treatment
of, and views about, gays and lesbians a problem for their faith
and for their relationships with people they care about, including gay and lesbian friends.

Many are leaving the Church, or at least evangelicalism, over the LGBT issue. According to Public Religion Research, 70 percent of America's most unchurched generation, the Millennials, say that "religious groups are alienating young people by being too judgmental about gay and lesbian issues," and 31 percent of those Millennials who have left the Church say this was an important factor in why they left. Go to PublicReligion.org (http://bit.ly/1DcHsz7) for more information.

Most younger Christians and ex-Christians have not come up with a biblical or theological alternative to the traditionalist position. But they are not satisfied at all with the status quo. And they sure want to be able to talk about the LGBT issue in some fresh ways, and in open, uncensored spaces. Anyone who works with young Christians has encountered these concerns.

Maybe what finally sent me over the edge at this particular meeting was that I didn't expect us to be talking about the LGBT issue. It wasn't on the agenda. But when first mentioned, I thought, for a hopeful nanosecond, that maybe I might hear some fresh ideas among these promising young leaders. But it was not to be. They mainly nodded sagely at each other as they passed around the same well-worn clichés that I have heard a thousand times. And so everyone emerged into the night air of New York City agreeing that they needed to keep fighting the good Christian fight against "the liberals and the gays," no matter how incomprehensible this view might be to most everyone else on those Manhattan streets.

Everyone agreed. Except me. I had found the "gay" parts of the conversation insufferable. It was fully clear to me at last that my mind had changed decisively on several aspects of this issue. I could no longer endure such conversations in silence. And I could not remain identified as an "evangelical" or especially as an "evangelical moral leader" if that meant an assumption that I shared the evangelical consensus on this issue. It was time to go public with some fresh thinking.

This is news if you know anything about evangelicalism, America's leading religious community by population, and an increasingly powerful force in global culture. This religious community, all around the world—think about some of the hateful legislation being advanced by evangelicals in Africa, for example—has almost unequivocally positioned itself as an opponent of gay rights and the gay community, and certainly as an opponent of any rethinking of traditional Christian sexual ethics in relation to gays and lesbians.

I myself have preached, lectured and written—politely, but still, I am on the record—in defense of the traditional evangelical position on these issues for as long as I have served as a Christian minister (27 years) and ethicist (21 years). I have stood before thousands of college and seminary students as a preacher and professor. I co-wrote perhaps the leading evangelical Christian ethics textbook (*Kingdom Ethics*, Intervarsity Press, 2003), which is read in nine languages around the world and takes the traditional position. Tens of thousands of Christians have read my words ...

This has not been a hobbyhorse issue for me. I have not traveled the country railing against "the homosexual lifestyle" or "the gay lobby." I have consistently attacked homophobia and called for Christian compassion. But I have said that there can be no moral acceptance of gay and lesbian sexual relationships. Until very recently, I had not written a word in favor of the full inclusion of gay and lesbian Christians in the Church. My adherence to the party line on this issue helped me have access to the leading evangelical colleges, seminaries, magazines, publishing houses and high-level Manhattan meetings that have been my privilege for two decades. I would name these connections to impress you with the extent to which I am deeply burrowed into the leading circles of my religious community but, well, that would be insufferable in its own way, don't you think? Check me out at www.davidpgushee. com or just take my word for it.

It certainly feels great to be a leader in one's profession, and the perks are nice too, including the travel, the royalties, and the sometimes quite comfortable hotel suites. And there's a special pride associated with being not just a leader, but a "religious leader." Such pride is very dangerous, though I can recognize it in myself and can see how it kept me quiet and still keeps many others from rocking the religious boat.

But that is what I must now do. Now I have something different to say. My mind has changed. This book is partly about the process through which my mind has changed, and partly about how I see biblical truth now that my mind has changed. In one sense it's a personal narrative; in another sense it's a statement of biblical theology as I see it now. I have been led on a journey that has put me in a very different place from where I started. It is only fair that everyone who has ever trusted what I wrote about this issue or any other issue in the past should be shown how it is that my mind has changed on this particular issue now. Any other interested person is warmly invited to listen in.

This book will describe how I have come to break with the evangelical consensus represented in that Manhattan meeting room. It is the story especially of how *not the Bible itself but traditionalist readings of certain texts in the Bible* have become increasingly implausible to me, while other texts about the Gospel message and the Church now seem to have a broader range of application, broad enough to include the full embrace of gays and lesbians.

My mind has changed—especially due to the transformative encounters I have been blessed to have with gay, lesbian, bisexual and transgender Christians over the last decade. One of them is my own beloved sister, who is dearer to me than words can say and who came out as a lesbian not long ago. Others are fellow church members. Some have been my students. Some were strangers who came looking for me and asking for a conversation by email, phone or over coffee.

As with straight Christians, the romantic-sexual lives of these LGBT Christians vary. Some are celibate. Some are not. Some are seeking relationships and some are not. Some believe same-sex relationships might be OK with God and some do not. Some are in covenant partnerships and some are not. Some are parents and some are not. I have learned from their great diversity never again to accept ill-informed statements about "the homosexual lifestyle."

The faith journeys and perspectives of these Christian friends vary in the same way. Some are liberal and some are conservative. Some are high church and some are low church. Some like hymns and some like praise choruses. They are just … Christian people, in all of their maddening and lovable diversity. Currently the most evangelistic friend I have is a gay Christian brother. He's always out there sharing his faith. Another gay Christian friend is into pop apocalyptic writings like the *Left Behind* series, which I personally loathe. And I have never seen a bigger collection of conservative Christian books than in the library of another gay Christian friend. When you actually allow gay and lesbian people into your life as a Christian, you are in for some surprises.

I did not go looking for these new friends, these experiences and encounters. They have come to me. I now believe that *they have been sent to me*. In my spiritual tradition, unexpected breakthroughs in Christian community are not viewed as accidental. They are more often described as the work of the Holy Spirit of God.

My mind and heart have changed as God has sent large numbers of "sexual others" into my life. These experiences have gradually led to a sharpening of my understanding of the Christian Gospel and the Christian Church, and some fresh thinking about what Christian sexual ethics should look like. I feel obligated before God and these new Christian friends of mine both to show you and tell you about this change, and, in all gentleness, to ask you to consider joining me on such a journey yourself.

What follows is not an exhaustive work. After various false starts I decided that the best way to address this subject was a series of short, timely chapters that anyone could read in relatively brief chunks of time. To use an older parallel, this is more like a collection of anti-slavery pamphlets than a ponderous scholarly tome. That is exactly how this collection was originally published, as a series of essays.

It is truly amazing how much scholarly ink has been spilled among specialists on parsing the finest details of Hebrew and Greek words and documents that might be relevant to this issue. No wonder laypeople are confused and don't know what to think. I hope that what I offer here will offer any reader fair-minded access to the main points of the scholarly discussion. But more importantly, I hope that at every point I direct attention to what is most deeply at stake. That is the Church's effort to discern what it means to follow Jesus in every area of life, including in our sexual ethics and in the way we treat sexual minorities in the Body of Christ.

CHAPTER 2

Our Moment: A Church With a Problem

The Church has a problem with gay and lesbian people.

IT SEEMS LIKE such a simple declaration. But that sentence could be read to mean so many different things. What did you hear?

1. The Church believes that same-sex acts and relationships are wrong.

2. The Church is facing problems because of its position on gays and lesbians and their relationships.

Or perhaps you quickly turned the sentence around, along these lines:

3. LGBT people have a problem with the Church.

Or maybe you got stuck on the terminology. You thought: this guy is all wrong already, because:

4. There is no such thing as "the Church."

All four possible readings of that opening sentence are true. At least, they are true enough to begin the conversation I want us to have together in this book.

So let's take them one at a time.

1. The Church believes that "homosexuality" (same-sex acts and relationships) is wrong.

Yes, it is true that until very recently the Christian church in all of its major branches included as part of its 2,000-year-old sexual morality a rejection of the moral legitimacy of sexual acts between persons of the same sex. (Did you see how carefully I stated that? Precision is needed when talking about these issues. Such precision is often hard to find—on any side of any issue—in an age when all arguments must be scaled to 140 tweetable characters.)

The Church never had a category called "sexual orientation" in its ancient tradition. Once it understood in the late 20th century that a distinction should be drawn between sexual orientation and sexual acts, the smarter branches of the Church were able to accept such a distinction. This helped some Christians tentatively begin to accept gay people in the Church, which was an advance. But it did not help them accept any moral legitimacy for any same-sex acts, and thus there could be no moral legitimacy for any gay or lesbian people engaged in, or even open to, romantic relationships.

The ancient Christian rejection of same-sex acts was just a small part of an elaborate sexual and family morality. That traditional morality focused on a man and woman making vows to God and each other to live out a lifetime marriage, and to restrict sexual activity to such a marriage, for better or for worse, in good times and bad. All sex outside of marriage was forbidden by the Church and believed to be against God's will. This older vision stressed the centrality of procreation and childrearing, viewing this sacred task as God's main purpose for marriage. Marriage was understood to be a divine sacrament, or at least a sacred covenant. Divorce and remarriage were either banned or tightly tied to specific offenses like adultery. The Church, at least in Christian-dominated societies, played a key role in teaching and socially enforcing its understanding of sexual morality and marriage, and there were few competitors to the Christian view.

Today, most people have very little exposure to a full pre-
sentation of the ancient Christian tradition about marriage,
family and sex, even if they attend a church on Sundays. Many
Christian preachers and teachers have lost contact with or
confidence in these ancient traditions. Or perhaps they fear
the wrath of their congregants, most of whom are out of com-
pliance with historic Christian sexual ethics in one way or
another. And so the preachers remain largely silent ...

Except perhaps about the LGBT issue. Here at least is one
aspect of historic Christian sexual morality that can still be
presented without offending too many people. Right? (One
wonders whether those preachers inveighing against gays and
lesbians would do so if they constituted 40 percent of their
congregants, as with divorce today.) And precisely because
so much of the rest of Christian sexual ethics has been abandoned, at least in practice, by Christians themselves, many
Christian leaders dig in all the more fiercely on same-sex relationships, viewing this as the final frontier, the last line of
defense.

Any adequate Christian thinking about the LGBT issue
needs to set the question back into its broader framework of
historic Christian sexual morality; and beyond that, into a far
broader Christian spiritual and theological context. That is
some of what I will do in this book.

But meanwhile, I grant the historical claim that the Church
has believed that same-sex acts and relationships are always
wrong, and I acknowledge that many millions of Christians
still believe this. In this sense, the Church does indeed have a
problem with gay and lesbian people and their relationships.

2. The Church is facing problems because of its position on
gays and lesbians and their relationships.

North American, Western European and generally cosmo-
politan opinion have in recent decades swung dramatically
against large parts of the Church's historic sexual morality,
including on same-sex relationships. One hundred years ago
same-sex acts were viewed as immoral, and often treated as

illegal, all over the western world. But that began changing during the late 20th century, and opinion has shifted dramatically in the last decade. State laws banning same-sex acts have been rejected by the U.S. Supreme Court, followed in recent years by the rapid spread of laws affirming same-sex marriage or at least blocking laws banning gay marriage. As of January, 2015, 70 percent of the U.S. population live in states where gay people can marry, and that number is likely to rise dramatically and quickly. And since the Supreme Court's 2013 rejection of the 1996 Defense of Marriage Act, the U.S. government has moved to treat gay and straight couples the same under federal law. The tides of change are flowing rapidly.

Pockets of Christian opinion, including some Protestant denominations and a variety of church and academic leaders, have made a doctrinal shift in recent decades on this issue. Many others have not made a doctrinal shift but have certainly shifted the spirit of their preaching, teaching and counsel toward more humane treatment of gay and lesbian persons.

But if the Church is understood to consist of three main ancient branches—Eastern Orthodox, Roman Catholic and Protestant—and if Protestant is understood to include two main communities today—the more progressive "mainline Protestants" and the more conservative evangelical Protestants—it is accurate to say that most of the Church has not made any kind of doctrinal shift. Eastern Orthodoxy, Roman Catholicism and Protestant evangelicalism have not changed the inherited Christian sexual ethic, while mainline Protestantism is bitterly divided, evidenced by constant fights over the issue at their summertime meetings.

This unwillingness or inability of most of the Church to change its sexual ethic (or especially to stop its sometimes hostile treatment of gay and lesbian people) has evoked enormous hostility from cultural leaders, gay rights activists, and millions of regular folks who feel they or their loved ones have been hurt by the Church. Many find the Church's posture and activities nothing but deplorable bigotry, little different than historic racism or sexism. The Church's image and evangelistic mission in U.S. culture have been damaged. The damage extends to many of the Church's own young people, who cringe every time the Church is identified as anti-gay, which seems to have become our defining characteristic. So the Church's stance on gay and lesbian people and their relationships, intended to advance Christian witness, has actually set its mission back among large numbers of people.

Cultural changes in recent years raise the prospect that Christians and institutions that hang onto traditional beliefs about the LGBT issue will eventually face total cultural rejection as well as significant legal problems. More and more often, leading Christians are "outed" for having at any time articulated traditionalist stands on same-sex issues, and are threatened with very visible forms of exclusion, such as when conservative pastor Louie Giglio was disinvited from praying at President Obama's second inauguration based on sermons he once preached. This sent a chill down the spine of every Christian leader who has ever offended current cultural standards in their preaching or writing on the LGBT issue. I am one such leader.

On the legal front, it is quite possible that conservative Christian universities with discriminatory policies related to gays and lesbians may one day lose the right to educate students who receive federal financial aid. It's a powerful lever—the percentage of "full-time undergraduates receiving financial aid … [reached] 85 percent in 2010," with much of this aid federally funded. (http://bit.ly/1127NSE) Such financial quarantining happened to segregationist Christian universities in the early 1970s when the Supreme Court ruled that racially discriminatory institutions could not have any contact with federal dollars. This same standard could one day be applied to Christian colleges vis-à-vis sexual-orientation discrimination. This could mean the death of some schools. The schools are very much aware of this even now; some are already joining legal battles to protect their right to

discriminate on the basis of religious conviction, while others
are trying to find a way to stand down.

Growing cultural hostility and imagined or real legal
threats are in turn evoking a siege mentality on the part of
many Christians, and certain highly visible conservative
Christian leaders are advancing this narrative with great skill.
Looking for historical precedents for moments in which "biblical" or "traditional" Christians have been attacked for their
heartfelt, non-negotiable beliefs, such Christians have found
solace in remembering periods of the persecution of the
Church. They remember the Church's suffering at the hands
of the Roman Empire, the Nazi regime in Germany, and the
communists in Eastern Europe and Asia. They fear it will soon
happen again, right here in America, and they are readying
themselves for a new era of persecution. Some Christian rhetoric is downright apocalyptic.

Of course, this posture assumes that all aspects of the traditional Christian position on the LGBT issue really are
non-negotiable Christian beliefs, similar to other non-ne-
gotiables Christians have suffered and died for in the past.
Ironically, *external* pressure on the Church has actually made
it much harder to have a serious *internal* Christian conversation on this very point. People on the defensive generally
hunker down rather than open up. This helps explain the
scene in the Manhattan conference room. The New York
venue was not coincidental in that sense. The more pressure
to change to fit the culture, the more Christians will just dig in
their heels. And in few places is there more pressure to change
Christian views than in New York.

Here is a warning to those from outside the Church who
despise traditional Christians for their sexual morality. The
faithful-witness-unto-death tradition in Christianity is a fearsome thing. Angry attacks on Christians for what they believe
to be unchangeable beliefs will mainly drive them into more
deeply entrenched resistance. *This dramatically increases the
responsibility of those of us within the community to have our*

own internal conversations about this issue. It might be wise
for outsiders to back off a bit while we do so, giving us some
space for the kind of organic change I am trying to advance in
this book. But still, those who are being discriminated against
don't really like to wait very long for those who are harming
them to figure out how to stop doing so. They won't wait forever. And they shouldn't have to.

3. LGBT people have a problem with the Church.

When same-sex love was "the love that dare not speak
its name," the vast majority of gay and lesbian people were
closeted. That meant the vast majority of straight people
never "knew" a gay person. It also meant that for centuries in
Church-dominated cultures, gay and lesbian people endured
in sad silence whatever the Church taught and did in relation
to them.

The loosening up of cultural attitudes has slowly brought
these silent sufferers out of the shadows. Some of us in Christian work, like me in my work as a pastor and professor, have
come to know gay, lesbian, bisexual and transgender Christians—committed, believing, baptized, morally serious
followers of Jesus. *There are millions of such "sexual other"*
Christians in the U.S. alone, and millions more around the
world. Say it with me: *There are millions of LGBT Christians.*
If we take the Christian population of the U.S. as 40 percent
of an overall population of 318 million, and then divide the
number of Christians in the United States by an LGBT population of about 4 percent, that gives us a conservative estimate
of five million such Christians in our country alone.

These Christians have been there all along. I have in recent
years met some of them. Until I began meeting them, I did
not know that these LGBT believers were already a part of the
Christian community. And their testimony is that they have
been badly hurt—sometimes by what the Church has taught
in pulpits and classrooms, sometimes by how it has been
taught, and sometimes by straight Christians who have felt

authorized to treat these (suspected) LGBT people with casual contempt, or worse.

So LGBT people have a problem with the Church. And those who love them have a problem with the Church that is at least as intense. This is not a perception problem, solvable by a rebranding campaign and a PR firm. This is a human suffering problem within the very heart of the Church. And many of those sufferers are very young. They are adolescents and young adults just now coming to terms with their sexuality. They are very badly wounded. Their suffering should matter to anyone with a shred of compassion for the suffering of the young. Which ought to include the Church. But perhaps ...

Did Christ Lie?

4. There is no such thing as "the Church."

I keep talking about the Church. But is there really such a thing as the Church, or are there instead just a myriad of "churches"? And should the focus really be on the Church as an institution, or instead on individual Christians, all of whom (should) come to their own beliefs about LGBT issues?

I am a Baptist minister and professor, and we Baptists tend to emphasize quite strongly the responsibility of all individual Christians to think carefully about issues of faith for ourselves, in obedience to Christ. We also emphasize what is called "congregational autonomy." Baptist churches don't follow a hierarchical chain of command and don't report up a ladder to bishops or cardinals or anyone else. Any look at the American religious landscape could easily conclude that a "Baptist" vision prevails here, whether congregations call themselves Baptist or not. A riot of congregational and individual versions of Christianity can be found all over the nation. Anybody can be a pastor and anybody can start a congregation, and any congregation can believe whatever the heck it wants to believe. *Except Christians*

It's a fact. And this does describe the chaotic American religious landscape pretty well. It's pretty crazy out there. But still, I chose the term "the Church" for this book quite intentionally. Even most congregationalists, whether we recite or even know the creeds, do believe in something like the "one, holy, catholic and apostolic Church," a phrase from the Nicene Creed. This means we implicitly or explicitly believe that ultimately the Church is "one" entity, founded by Jesus; it is "holy" in its origin and holy in its aims and seeks to be holy in its conduct; it is "catholic," which means universal, with an existence crossing and including just about every tribe, nation and language group; and it is "apostolic," traceable to Jesus and his original apostles and continuing over 2,000 years until now.

If this is true, leaders of the Church today such as myself and many readers of this book carry profound responsibilities to the one, holy, catholic and apostolic Church. We can't simply abandon the Bible, or Church tradition, or historic Christian beliefs, just because there is a cultural movement of great power bearing down hard on us to snap our views into line with prevailing opinion. This is precisely what Church leaders (at their best) have refused to do—from ancient Rome to Nazi Germany to apartheid South Africa. This steadfast *saying no to culture in order to say yes to Jesus Christ* was precisely what they were obligated to do by their responsibilities as Christian leaders.

Today's Church leaders face the same kinds of responsibilities. We must get Jesus-following right in our time as earlier Church leaders did in theirs. We are accountable to every prior Christian generation—and certainly to the Lord of the Church, Jesus Christ.

So I write this book—this may not sound modest, but I am trying to be clear—self-consciously as an ordained Christian minister and widely published Christian moral leader with grave responsibilities to God and the Church universal. You will hear me say no to culture at least as much as I say yes here, because my goal is not to accommodate culture, but to meet my responsibilities before God as a Christian leader.

As such, in this book *I am asking whether the Church should change our mind and our practices in relation to Christian LGBT people and their relationships—not because we are under*

*pressure from a hostile culture to do so, but because within the
terms of our own faith we might now conclude that this is one
of those cases in 2,000 years of Christian history where we have
gotten some things wrong.*

Revising any significant aspect of Christian tradition is a
tall order. This helps to explain why serious Church bodies are
not changing their views rapidly. They cannot be expected to
do so if they have any sense of organic relation with their own
intellectual heritage or any meaningful connection with the
Church universal. If we don't get to just make this stuff up as
we go along, changing our mind must be a careful and deliber-
ative process, not a hasty surrender to culture's latest demands.
In that sense, Christianity, like most religious traditions of any
vintage, is inherently conservative. Change happens slowly.

And yet, because many Christians and Church leaders
sense that something is not quite right—that our tradition
has not adequately understood either itself or the contemporary sexual others in our midst—we sense that some kind of
change is needed. We just don't know how to get there. And so
we seethe in conflict and confusion. We can't quite change our
mind, but we are not fully comfortable with where we are. We
keep picking at this scab without really getting anywhere. And
so even when the issue is not on the agenda, it always surfaces.

Notice that I use the singular "mind," not the plural "minds,"
here and in the title of this book. That's because I believe the
question that matters is whether *the collective mind of the
Church universal can and ought to change.* The issue is not
whether some Christians as individuals change their minds,
but whether the Church universal will or should change
its mind collectively. And that takes disciplined reflection
together, in community, with all hands on deck making their
best contribution.

Using the tools most central to our own Christian faith
tradition, I will make a case *for changing our mind.* Not on
everything we have ever taught, by any means. Indeed, I will
try to show that *to transform how LGBT people are treated*

by and in the Church is not in fact to change our mind but
instead to change our attitude and practice in a manner fully
consistent with historic Christian convictions about the Gospel and the Church. A church that offers hospitable welcome
to gay people, lesbians and sexual others as grateful recipients
of God's saving love in Jesus Christ is in fact a church faithful to the Gospel and what it means to be the Church. Much
needed change, I will argue, can take place without reconsidering the sexual ethics issues at all.

I will then make the more difficult case that *a change in just
one dimension of our thinking about Christian sexual morality* can be considered within the terms of Christian Scripture.
This change could invite every adult Christian to bring their
romantic-sexual commitments into the demanding covenantal
structure of historic Christian sexual morality. And for those
who find this a bridge too far, the Church at least can demon-
strate the capacity to live in community with each other even
if we find full agreement impossible on this question.

Everything that I offer here will reflect the changing of
heart and mind that I myself have undergone in the last 10
years. That Christian ethics textbook that I mentioned earlier
has helped to establish me as one of global evangelicalism's
leading moral thinkers. I find that I now cannot fully endorse
the few pages I wrote there about the LGBT issue. That will
shock some people. I want to take you on the journey from
Kingdom Ethics to *Changing Our Mind*.

One last thing: The U.S. and many other countries are
experiencing agonizing debates over gay rights. As I write,
the hottest current social debate in our nation is over gay
marriage.

But this book is not mainly about America or about legal
rights for gay people. My intent is to think about Gospel
truths. American Christians are so accustomed to cultural
dominance that if we think that God has banned—or mandated—something, then we think we should try to ban or
mandate it in the state. Our own (fading) cultural dominance

in the U.S., together with theological sloppiness easily confuses us here.

What the state of Florida or Minnesota or Iowa or the U.S. Government does about recognizing gay people as married is important. But it is not a first-order Christian theology or ethics question. It is a state question, and the way the state resolves such questions differs foundationally from the way the Church reasons about its doctrine and inner life. When the state thinks about marriage, it is mainly attempting to account for the public interest with regard to such matters as tax status, property rights and child custody disputes upon divorce. In fact, the vast majority of the content of state marriage laws has to do with divorce, not marriage itself. (Trust me, I've studied state marriage laws. They're depressing.) It is appalling that the Church and its representatives have allowed state debates over marriage to preempt and dominate our own thinking about the whole range of concerns related to LGBT people in the life of the Church.

What we discover about Christian fidelity to Jesus certainly will be relevant to our witness to the state. But the fundamental need right now for Christians is to think seriously about whether the Church's own marginalized sexual minorities will be treated, unequivocally, as sisters and brothers in Christ. That is the work I want us to do together here. I actually think that getting this right in the Church will be our greatest contribution to society.

my concern is not so much in what the state allows) but that in their zeal to make it allowable they me/demanded that the church change its beliefs. In doing thes the state is, in my view) establishing a state religon.

CHAPTER 3

Starting a Conversation

*Every generation has its hot-button
issue. For us, it's the LGBT issue.*

EVERYWHERE I GO, I run into the LGBT issue, whether
I feel like running into it or not. You may feel the same way.
And everywhere, it creates conflict.

It surfaces and creates conflict in nearly every single day's
religion and/or politics news. Today's news.

It surfaces and creates conflict in many, many denominations and fellowships. My fellowship.

It surfaces and creates conflict in many, many congregations. My congregation.

It surfaces and creates conflict in many, many classrooms.
My classroom.

It surfaces and creates conflict in many, many families. My
family.

Everywhere I go, I run into three different kinds of
responses to the LGBT issue:

1. Some want to hold onto what they understand to be
traditional Christian and/or cultural attitudes and practices
toward some things, or everything, associated with the LGBT
issue, including biblical interpretations, church practices, cultural attitudes, and state/national laws. As a group, let's call
these the *traditionalists*, even though dramatic social, scientific

and religious changes in recent decades mean that our current sexuality-talk actually doesn't have that long of a tradition.

2. Some want to see change happen in biblical interpretations, church practices, cultural attitudes, and state/national laws, in search of at least a more humane context (or much more) for LGBT people to live their lives. As a group, let's call these advocates for change the *revisionists*, though with the same caveat as just above.

3. Most want to avoid talking about this issue for as long as possible, if at all possible, until it becomes impossible. *Avoiders* want to evade the subject for a wide variety of reasons, including genuine convictional uncertainty, fear of hurting people and fear of conflict and schism.

A spectrum can also be identified in terms of the *intensity* with which people approach this issue, ranging from very low to extremely high—though in general if someone is writing or doing activism about this issue, they are not on the low end of the intensity scale. For example, avoiders are often quite intense in their desire to avoid the issue altogether, often linked to their responsibility for holding institutions together or keeping their jobs.

In this series of brief chapters, I will reflect on the multifaceted LGBT issue. I hope to provide some helpful commentary for others who might like to get past avoidism and move toward some convictional clarity, and hope to do so using a methodology that is recognizable and usable by other Christians. Perhaps I can identify some "forks in the road" (look for that phrase, it will be important when it appears) and other useful road markers that can help readers think through their own views.

For those not paying close attention to developments in the Christian conversation about this issue, the past decade has seen a dramatic shift in the intellectual and ecclesial terrain. A substantial scholarly and popular literature is developing, not just in the older ecumenical/liberal conversation (four decades old at least), but also in the evangelical/conservative precincts of American Christianity.

Notably, evangelical Christianity is producing a first-generation of revisionist or quasi-revisionist literature—much of it popular, a bit of it by scholars and some of it written by self-identified LGBT evangelicals. This new literature is generating resistance among those who seek to refute the particular claims of evangelical revisionists and who try to define them *ipso facto* as no longer evangelical, or Christian.

If you have not heard of Jenell Williams Paris (http://amzn. to/1127Myf), Andrew Marin (http://bit.ly/1127Myj), Matthew Vines (http://bit.ly/1127NSL), Wesley Hill (http://amzn. to/1127MOC), Justin Lee (http://bit.ly/1127MOD), Jeff Chu (http://bit.ly/1127NSU), James Brownson (http://amzn. to/Zj2pcv), Ken Wilson (http://amzn.to/Zj2n4e), Mark Achtemeier (http://bit.ly/Zj2pcy), and Wendy VanderWal-Gritter, it is time to change that.[2]

---

2 Jenell Williams Paris, *The End of Sexual Identity: Why Sex Is Too Important to Define Who We Are* (Downers Grove, IL: Intervarsity Press, 2011); Andrew Marin, *Love is an Orientation: Elevating the Conversation with the Gay Community* (Downers Grove, IL: Intervarsity Press, 2009); Matthew Vines, *God and the Gay Christian: The Biblical Case in Support of Same-Sex Relationships* (New York: Convergent Books, 2014); Wesley Hill, *Washed and Waiting: Reflections on Christian Faithfulness and Homosexuality* (Grand Rapids: Zondervan, 2010); Justin Lee, *Torn: Rescuing the Gospel from the Gays-vs.-Christians Debate* (New York: Jericho Books, 2012); Jeff Chu, *Does Jesus Really Love Me? A Gay Christian's Pilgrimage in Search of God in America* (New York: HarperCollins, 2013); James V. Brownson, *Bible, Gender, Sexuality: Reframing the Church's Debate on Same-Sex Relationships* (Grand Rapids: William B. Eerdmans Publishing Company, 2013); Ken Wilson, *A Letter to my Congregation: An evangelical pastor's path to embracing people who are gay, lesbian and transgender into the company of Jesus* (Canton, MI: Read the Spirit Books, 2014); Mark Achtemeier, *The Bible's Yes to Same-Sex Marriage: An Evangelical's Change of Heart* (Louisville: Westminster John Knox

The fact that gay people, indeed, gay *evangelical* Christians, are no longer just being talked *about*, but finding their own voices, and making scriptural and theological and ethical arguments for themselves, inevitably changes the nature of the conversation—if we are willing to have a conversation. It is harder to simply dehumanize and dismiss a flesh-and-blood human being with a name and a family and a history of serving Christ in the local church.

Every generation has its hottest of all hot-button issues, the issue that becomes the litmus test of everyone's orthodoxy and provokes conflicts sometimes leading to schism. In earlier generations it was slavery, or segregation, or apartheid, or Nazism, or abortion, or temperance, or Sabbath or tongue-speaking. I am old enough to have lived through the 1980s/1990s fight over women's roles in the Church among Baptists and evangelicals, which led more than one congregation and denomination into schism. This LGBT issue, 25 years later, is doing the same thing. Odd, really—the big divisive issue in our messed up world today is how perhaps one-twentieth of all people handle their sexuality. That fact itself is remarkable. What does it say about our priorities that we will fight to the death over this issue rather than, say, divide over our stand on clergy sex abuse or mass murder or caring for the poor?

Still, this is the issue of the moment, and many are pressing for serious but nonfundamentalist Christians to end their silence about it, and to do so with theological-ethical precision and depth. There comes a moment when avoidism cannot be sustained due to Christian missional, vocational and leadership responsibility, as well as our Christian obligations toward vulnerable human beings. I hope my explorations can be helpful to individuals and churches seeking a way forward.

Press, 2014); Wendy VanderWal-Gritter, *Generous Spaciousness: Responding to Gay Christians in the Church* (Grand Rapids: Brazos, 2014).

CHAPTER 4

What Exactly Is the Issue?

How and why historic Christian understandings of sexuality are being re-evaluated today.

SO: WHAT EXACTLY is the issue that everyone is fighting about?

One starting point might be to say that historic Christian understandings of sexuality are being re-evaluated due to evidence offered in the lives of those who do not fit the historic heterosexual norm, together with associated research and mental health efforts.

The historic Christian sexual norm was exclusively heterosexual. (Some call it heteronormative, or more pejoratively, heterosexist.) It declared that all human beings exist in two distinct sexes, male and female, and that they are divinely commanded to have sexual relations only with the opposite sex. Furthermore, the Church taught that sexual behavior should be constrained to lifetime monogamous marriages and, often, emphasized procreation as the central divine purpose for sexual activity. This heterosexual-marital-procreative norm was also generally linked to a patriarchal understanding of gender—that is, differences in men's and women's (divinely prescribed) roles and behaviors—that gave men greater power. The Bible was, and still is, cited as authority for some or all of these norms related to gender and sexuality. A wide range of associated cultural and legal practices reflected and reinforced these theological and ethical beliefs once Christianity became the official or dominant religion in many lands, as it did here in the United States.

These powerful sex-and-gender paradigms have been challenged in many ways in recent decades. Many of our most intense religious and "culture war" battles have been fought on this broad front between advocates and resisters of change. (Failure to disentangle and treat specific issues separately has engendered unnecessary confusion and conflict. More on this later.)

Our topic in this book, of course, is the particular challenge to the norm offered by the discovery/acknowledgment of a persistent presence in human societies of women and men who experience permanent, exclusive same-sex attraction rather than opposite-sex attraction—as well as those who report attraction to both sexes; or fluid desire patterns; or biologically indeterminate or uncertain gender identity. Several recent studies for the U.S. suggest a lesbian, gay, bisexual or transgender population ranging from 3.4 to 5 percent.

If they have not been simply ostracized or rejected outright, young adults reporting any level of same-sex attraction, especially in religiously conservative families and congregations, often have been told (amidst their own great spiritual and psychological distress) that their "struggle with their sexuality" can be resolved through prayer, repentance, moral effort, or therapies designed to change their sexual orientation. They often have also been told that their continued acceptance in family or religious life requires (the success of) such efforts. Probably many readers personally know people—I certainly do—who have attempted without success and with terrible suffering to change their sexual orientation under external or self-imposed religious pressure, perhaps through some form of sexual-orientation-change therapy. One heartrending collection of such testimonies is in Mitchell Gold and Mindy Drucker's book, *Crisis*, but there are many others.[3]

However, the total failure of the "ex-gay" movement—as evidenced most recently by Exodus International's closure and apology (http://cnn.it/1wJY7pE) in 2013 and its leader Alan Chambers' statement the year before that "99.9%" of the people they had tried to help had not experienced a change in their sexual orientation (http://bit.ly/Zj2pcA)— has destroyed the plausibility of such efforts. Already in 2009, the American Psychological Association (http://bit. ly/1wJY6BX) and U.K. Royal College of Psychiatrists (http:// bit.ly/Zj2n4k) warned against sexual-orientation-change efforts as harmful, and some U.S. states are now moving to outlaw them altogether (http://bit.ly/Zj2n4m). It is hard to see how responsible Christian ministries can any longer offer, or refer to, sexual-orientation-change therapy. Several recent books have been written by those with experience in these ministries, who have abandoned them or utterly transformed their approach.[4]

Research and clinical results such as these have prompted a dramatic reconceiving of sexuality in the social and behavioral sciences and the mental health professions.

The accounts offered in widely used psychology textbooks, such as the text offered by David Myers, reflect current research.[5]

3 Mitchell Gold with Mindy Drucker, *Crisis: 40 Stories Revealing the Personal, Social, and Religious Pain and Trauma of Growing Up Gay in America* (Austin, TX: Greenleaf Book Group Press, 2008); Bernadette Barton, *Pray the Gay Away: The Extraordinary Lives of Bible Belt Gays* (New York/London: New York University Press, 2012).

4 Wendy VanderWal-Gritter, *Generous Spaciousness: Responding to Gay Christians in the Church* (Grand Rapids: Brazos, 2014); Jeremy Marks, *Exchanging the Truth of God for a lie: One man's spiritual journey to find the truth about homosexuality and same-sex partnerships*, 2nd Edition (Glasgow: Bell & Bain, 2009).

5 David G. Myers, *Psychology*, 10th Edition (New York: Worth Publishers, 2013), pp. 427-434.

Myers begins by accepting human sexual-orientation diversity as a fact. He distinguishes between *sexual orientation*—the direction of enduring sexual-romantic desire and attraction, largely biological in origin; *sexual identity*—socially influenced self-understanding/labeling; and *sexual behavior*—choices and patterns in sexual activity. He notes the crucial role of culture in creating a context either for rejecting or accepting those of different sexual orientations, concluding: "Yet whether a culture condemns or accepts homosexuality, heterosexuality prevails and homosexuality survives." Myers claims that "sexual orientation in some ways is like handedness: Most people are one way, some the other. A very few are truly ambidextrous. Regardless, the way one is endures."[6]

Myers, by the way, is an evangelical Christian who teaches at Hope College in Michigan, a winsome evangelical school in the Dutch Reformed tradition.

Even if one accepts the claims of psychologists like David Myers, it does not resolve theological and moral questions raised by Scripture and the Christian tradition. It does, however, give us a crucial understanding without which we cannot adequately wrestle with those theological and moral questions. Perhaps this is the first major fork in the road: Some will take the personal narratives, psychological research, and clinical conclusions just outlined seriously, integrating them into further Christian reflection and ministry, and others might choose to dismiss them. I cannot take the latter path.

Next, I will explore how traditionalist Christian communities and their leaders are currently attempting to navigate these waters. The picture is much more complex than you might think.

---

6 David G. Myers, *Psychology*, 10th Edition (New York: Worth Publishers, 2013), p. 428.

CHAPTER 5

Change We Can All Support

*Much has changed for LGBT people in America
since Anita Bryant and Jerry Falwell days—
change we all can support, I hope.*

I HAVE CLAIMED that contemporary behavioral scientists and mental health experts have responded to research evidence, and the lives of LGBT people, by reconceptualizing human sexuality.

I suggested that there is a fork in the road here, between accepting these relatively new but firmly held clinical claims about sexual orientation and refusing to do so. I also acknowledged that the acceptance of research/clinical/factual claims does not resolve moral issues—though it should inform moral reasoning. There is a difference between descriptive-level claims and prescriptive-level claims, as I often teach my students. Descriptive claims describe what is going on; prescriptive claims prescribe actions and offer moral norms.

∾

In these next two chapters, I want to explore the sometimes-surprising trajectory of responses in recent years to the LGBT issue on the Christian traditionalist side; that is, among those who continue to believe and teach exclusively heterosexual-marital sexual ethics. The landscape has changed in positive ways for gay people, changes that are important to notice.

When the first major call for social equality for gays and lesbians began to be heard in the United States in the 1970s, Christian resistance was fierce. It is instructive to remember the voices of people like Anita Bryant, who for a few years led a ferocious anti-gay campaign (http://bit.ly/1127O9l) that was picked up later by Tim LaHaye and others. Opposition to gay rights was deep and pervasive in the agenda of the Christian Right, and many of us still remember the way gay people were blamed by some for bringing divine judgment on America (http://abcn.ws/1127MON) through such disasters as 9/11 and Katrina.

Westboro Baptist Church (http://bit.ly/1DcHuaj) has provided a horrifying example of the continued survival of "Christian" contempt for gay and lesbian people, but their very marginality has been instructive evidence of progress elsewhere.

Some Christians once saw discrimination against gays in employment, government and military service, housing, adoption rights, and other sectors as a righteous crusade. All kinds of demeaning rhetoric was employed about gays, sometimes from the pulpit. This overall climate contributed to the conditions for much derogatory everyday language about gay people, or people who "seemed" gay, or who "looked" gay, as well as other forms of direct and indirect bullying, including of children. What was proclaimed loftily from the pulpit was all too often translated less loftily on the playground.

I remember one incident quite vividly: I was at a minor league baseball game, about 10 years ago. A player on the opposing team had a last name that was very similar to a commonly employed derogatory term for gay men that I am unwilling to put in print. Every time he came up to bat, he was serenaded by a group of clean-cut young men near the third-base dugout. They simply sang out his name, over and over, in

order to make fun of him, and by extension every person who
has ever been called by that particular anti-gay slur.

I learned later that these clean-cut young men were frater-
nity brothers at a nearby Christian college.

I am not at all saying that the situation has been transformed, or that LGBT people no longer experience any of
these things, or that there aren't still plenty of Christians who
might pull that kind of stunt.

But still, the landscape has changed dramatically. The vast
majority of Christians who could be classified as traditionalists on the LGBT issue have backpedaled considerably from
the claims and behaviors of the Anita Bryant era. This is all to
the good.

Breaking sharply with the past, though usually without
acknowledging any movement in their own position, leaders
of many traditionalist Christian communities or institutions
do their best to avoid verbally stigmatizing or demonizing
gays and lesbians, as their forebears did not so long ago.

Previous public policy and culture fights that traditionalist Christians once led have almost been forgotten. Remember
the Disney boycott? (http://cnn.it/1127MOQ) The Tele-
tubbies? (http://nyti.ms/1127O9s) The fight over gays in
the military? (http://abt.cm/1127OpH) These once gained
national headlines. On these, traditionalist Christians have
largely gone silent.

After the bruising civil gay-marriage battles of recent years,
some traditionalist Christian leaders acknowledge that on
the cultural and legal front, at least for now, their side is losing (http://bit.ly/1DcHsPH). Some are suggesting (http://bit.
ly/1127PKq) that the fights over gay marriage are doing the
Church's mission more harm than good, and that it is time to
fall back from that struggle.

This helps explain the newfound focus on religious lib-
erty for traditionalists; it is a fallback position. It represents
retrenchment. The chorus now seems to be: "If we can't win
the culture, we can at least protect our right to dissent."

Change is happening in relation to the clinical and scientific claims as well, undoubtedly related to straight people getting to know lesbian and gay people. In 1993, 22 percent of Americans reported having a close friend or family member who was gay or lesbian. In 2013, that number had risen to 65 percent (http://bit.ly/1127PKr). It is making a big difference.

More and more traditionalist Christians now accept, however reluctantly, that a small number of human beings simply are of same-sex orientation. Fewer make the ungrounded claim that sexual orientation is willful perversity, chosen and changeable. Many traditionalist Christians understand that millions of their neighbors have adopted a sexual identity as lesbian, gay or bisexual, and that these core self-identities point to something real and significant that it is counterproductive to ignore—even if the whole concept of sexual identity can be challenged as a modern construct.[7]

And more and more traditionalist Christians have gay friends. These trends are especially clear among younger Christians (http://bit.ly/1127PKr).

And so, it is increasingly agreed, even on the traditionalist Christian side: gay people exist. It is wrong to call them names or use slurs about them. Their relationships should not be criminalized. They should not be discriminated against in employment, housing and public accommodation. They should not be bullied. They should never have to be afraid of violence as they go about their daily lives. They should not be blamed for America's security problems or social ills. They should not be stigmatized or treated with contempt. There should be no space in church life or culture for their dehumanization and mistreatment.

Any Christian reader, anywhere in the world, *regardless of your views on Christian sexual ethics,* ought to be able

---

7 Jenell Williams Paris, *The End of Sexual Identity: Why Sex Is Too Important to Define Who We Are* (Downers Grove, IL: Intervarsity Press, 2011).

to agree with that last paragraph. If you do agree, you already support significant change from what the Christian status quo was not so long ago.

CHAPTER 6

Gay Christians Exist

*How even ardent traditionalists now acknowledge
the existence of gay Christians.*

WHILE SOME TRADITIONALIST voices still dispute it,
more are willing to acknowledge that the LGBT community
contains a sizable population of professing Christians. However one defines a Christian—by baptism, by stated personal
commitment to Jesus Christ, by visible spiritual practices and
gifts, or by church membership, attendance, and service—
there are indeed millions of LGBT Christians, and many more
who were once Christians but have become alienated from the
Church.

Many have made this acknowledgment of the existence of
gay Christians through personal experience. I, for one, have
been deeply changed, not just by meeting and getting to know
numerous gay Christians, but by discovering that some of
them are theologically more conservative than I am. My once
unthinking connection between "gay" and "liberal"—so common in traditionalist circles—has collapsed under the weight
of the evidence.

I am not the only one who has reached this particular fork
in the road.

One indicator of dramatic change among traditionalist
Christians is that the go-to voices for many conservatives and

evangelicals on the LGBT issue today have become openly gay
but celibate Christians. A good example is Wesley Hill, a professor at the evangelical Trinity School for Ministry and author
of *Washed and Waiting*.[8]

Often, the reviewers of books on LGBT issues in flagship
evangelical publications like *Christianity Today* are now celibate gay Christians like Hill, not straight folks. This certainly
seems like at least an implicit endorsement, as if that very
careful evangelical magazine is saying: Yes indeed, there are
gay Christians, and as long as they are celibate, they are in per-
fectly good standing with us.

This change is reflected in a fascinating terminolog-
ical development in the evangelical conversation. This
involves delineating between "Side A" and "Side B" (http://bit.
ly/1127PKs) Christians, a distinction that originally emerged
in the internal gay Christian dialogue.

While recognizing the reality of sexual orientation, Side
A Christians believe it is possible for gay believers to enter
covenantal same-sex relationships with God's blessing. Side
B folks believe God does not ever bless same-sex relationships. Online and in venues like the Gay Christian Network
(http://bit.ly/1127MOD) annual conference, these two sides
get together and attempt to be in Christian community and
support each other. Straight Christians could learn from the
forbearance displayed by these gay Christians, who have so
much more at stake on this issue than the rest of us do.[9]

I have learned never to assume a person's "position" on the
morality of LGBT relationships based on their stated sexual
orientation or identity. I know straight Christians who take
Side A when it comes to covenantal gay relationships, and gay
Christians who take Side B out of what they understand God

---

8 Wesley Hill, *Washed and Waiting: Reflections on Christian
Faithfulness and Homosexuality* (Grand Rapids: Zondervan, 2010).
9 See Justin Lee, a Side A gay Christian and author of *Torn: Rescuing
the Gospel from the Gays-vs.-Christians Debate* (New York: Jericho
Books, 2012).

requires. To add another wrinkle, I know avowedly gay-orien-
tation Christians who are in heterosexual marriages in which
their spouse knows of their sexual orientation. Pastors min-
istering in this arena need to be aware of these complexities.
Good theological/pastoral education still matters.

We have come a long way since 1964, when mainline minister Robert Cromey was vilified and threatened within his
denomination for even meeting with gay people, and when
sneering contempt, potential imprisonment and brutal violence toward gay people were often the norm. (The situation
remains that terrible in other parts of the world, however,
including in Africa, where retrograde Christianity is playing
a major role. The contrast with the generally more polite U.S.
discussion today is itself instructive.)

What sexual ethicist James Nelson once called the "reject-
ing-punitive" (http://bit.ly/1127OpO) position toward gay
people has weakened on the home front. Still, when families
reject their own children, whether punitively or nonpunitively,
it remains hugely damaging, as many heartrending accounts
of family-exiled gay teenagers and gay suicides indicate. (On
this point, check out the important work of the Family Acceptance Project. (http://bit.ly/1127OpR)) I learned recently that
a group called Lost-N-Found in my own Atlanta community
has opened a shelter for homeless gay adolescents (http://bit.
ly/1127OpT), exiled from their families. One can only weep
that this is even necessary. It is fair to say that even as some
traditionalist Christian leaders retreat to the "affirm-the-celi-
bate-gay" Side B line, many in the Christian grassroots are not
getting that message, to the great suffering of their own children. *It says something really terrible when the least safe place
to deal with sexual orientation and identity issues is the Christian family and church.*

Still, in more sophisticated Christian conversations today,
including among many on the traditionalist side, the LGBT
issue is not couched any longer in the language of deviance
and hellfire, with the word "gay" or "homosexual" little more

than an epithet. Instead, it is this: If we acknowledge the existence of a small but persistent percentage of the human—and Christian—community that is not heterosexual, or solely heterosexual, what do we do now? How shall LGBT Christians be integrated within congregational life? What does the Gospel say and require? Can the exegetical and sexual ethics questions be reopened at all? Who has the authority to make these determinations? And where is God in all of this?

These will be subjects of later reflection. But *regardless of your stance on the sexual ethics issues,* if you have stayed with me so far, I hope you will agree that all Christians ought to be eager to offer well-informed understanding and hospitality to people of non-heterosexual orientation and identity in our families and churches. Anything short of that is not consistent with the requirements of the Gospel.

CHAPTER 7

Six Options for the Churches

*Six options for how a church responds to the
arrival of gay couples in its midst.*

WHAT IS THE posture that forgiven sinners in the church
should have toward other forgiven sinners?

Pope Francis rocked the Christian world with his response
in a 2013 interview when he was asked about celibate gay
priests in the Roman Catholic Church. His actual quote was
this: "If someone is gay, who searches for the Lord and has
goodwill, who am I to judge?" (http://bit.ly/1127OpY)

It was quickly made clear by the Vatican that the pope was
not signaling a change in Catholic moral theology. But he was
signaling a change in papal moral tone. This pope would lead
with a welcome emphasis on humility, service and love, not
judgment and condemnation. The pope accepted that there
are gay Christians and that they belong in the church family—
even if there can be no reconsideration of Christian sexual
ethics.

So let's say a congregation dips its toes in the water here by
welcoming celibate gay Christians to membership and unhindered involvement in the congregation. Then, however, the
word gets out that this congregation is a safe and friendly
place for gay Christians. Soon a covenanted or even married

gay couple present themselves for membership, perhaps not knowing that a formal or informal moral line on this issue exists precisely at this point. If they are accepted into membership, maybe one or two more couples come along. This is probably inevitable, because many gay Christians are looking for a safe place to (re-)enter a Christian community, and when they find one, they invite their friends. And most lesbian and gay Christians are not committed to celibacy, just as most straight Christians are not celibates. Celibacy has always been an exceptional and rare calling in the Christian church.

And so it is just about at this point that the rest of us pastor-/church leader-/church people-types will not be able to avoid figuring out what we should do and say in response.

Here are six options:

1. **The "ask no questions" option.** Some churches default to welcoming covenanted gay couples without dealing with the relevant ethical issues at all, either from the pulpit or anywhere else. If a church's overall policy on membership does not involve moral examination or church accountability, it would hardly make sense to begin doing it just with this population and on this issue. (Though, of course, this is often what happens, leaving the congregation wide open to the charge of selective moralism.)

2. **The "who are we to judge?" option**. Some churches implicitly or explicitly take the position that the church is a "field hospital" (another image Pope Francis has used) for wounded sinners, of which each of us is the chief, rather than a community of the perfect. Therefore our default posture is: Who are we to judge—when someone comes into the Christian community—even if they are involved in a relationship which some of us might think is sinful? This is a posture of *each of us withholding judgment on anybody except for ourselves.* Who are you to judge the servant of another? (Romans

14:4) We are doing our own log-in-our-eye removal work all the time, making us too busy to point out the speck in the other's eye (Matthew 7:1-5).

3. **The "dialogue for discernment" option**. Some churches now say that the moral status before God of covenanted gay relationships is uncertain, or that opinion within the Christian community and our congregation is unsure or divided. They declare a period of dialogue for discernment, a time of listening together, sometimes inviting or welcoming interested LGBT neighbors and/ or Christians, including couples, into the dialogue. Or, going a bit further, like evangelicals Ken Wilson and Wendy VanderWal-Gritter, some declare this a "disputable matter" in Romans 14 terms and decide to live together in a forbearing and loving community despite long-term differences of conviction.[10]

We certainly need good models of dialogue on this issue.[11]

---

10 Ken Wilson, *A Letter to my Congregation: An evangelical pastor's path to embracing people who are gay, lesbian and transgender into the company of Jesus* (Canton, MI: Read the Spirit Books, 2014), pp. 104-110. Wendy Vander Wal-Gritter, *Generous Spaciousness: Responding to Gay Christians in the Church* (Grand Rapids: Brazos, 2014), ch. 11; Andrew Marin, *Love is an Orientation: Elevating the Conversation with the Gay Community* (Downers Grove, IL: Intervarsity Press, 2009). Note that the framing of dialogue is shifting rapidly—from "Christians" dialoguing with "the gay community" to an internal Christian conversation among gay and straight fellow-believers.
11 Check out Ted Grimsrud and Mark Thiessen Nation, *Reasoning Together: A Conversation on Homosexuality* (Scottdale, PA: Herald Press, 2008). It reflects the authors' Mennonite peaceableness. We could all learn from them.

4. The "pastoral accommodation" option. Some churches implicitly or explicitly take the position that while God's (original/pre-fall/best/intended) plan for sexuality is heterosexual monogamous lifetime marriage, the contemporary church is full of people at all times who are falling short of that plan—as we fall short in every area of life, such as, for example, anger, or greed, or vengeance, or gluttony. So the church and its pastors are constantly making pastoral accommodations to the realities of life in a fallen world.

It is certainly true, for example, that Jesus' teaching on divorce (Matthew 19:1-12 and Mark 10:1-12), hardly makes room for the mass divorce on grounds of incompatibility that we find in our culture. Yet the Church—including most traditionalist churches, which have been backpedaling for years on this one—accommodates many individuals and couples who are on their second or third divorce and/or marriage. And this is not even to speak about the gaps in adherence to the "sex-within-marriage-only" ethic on the part of heterosexual singles, especially with the rapid rise in cohabitation.

The pastoral decision to seek to minister healing and direction to such couples *where they are*, even if it is not "God's best" as designed, could be extended to gay and lesbian couples.

Notice that these first four options require no direct reconsideration of Christian moral tradition or sexual ethics. They raise ecclesiological questions more than anything else, especially the question of whether churches are capable of or even interested in practicing any form of accountable membership or church discipline. But that issue is a perennial one in church life.

Here is another fork in the road.

Options 1 through 4 represent at least a temporary terminus point on the LGBT issue for those churches or Christians that take those paths. We don't ask questions; we don't judge others; we are dialoguing about this, or consider this a disputable matter; we are doing pastoral accommodation to a church-full of broken people. Meanwhile, y'all come, and we'll figure it out together with God's help. If churches could be explicit about which path they are taking it would remove a lot of uncertainty for everyone.

Churches could do far worse than this. For example, to avoid the issue altogether, they could do what some churches still do:

5. **The "exclusionist" option.** Some churches simply refuse admission to church membership for any gay person (even if celibate), or more often, draw the line at welcoming noncelibate gays, such as gay couples. Let's call these "5a" and "5b." But then when someone's child turns out to be gay, there is no way to avoid the issue within the congregation other than to exile them from the Church unless they commit to celibacy. And these churches often turn out to have closeted gay members in them, because that 3.4 to 5 percent of the population is found in these congregations too.

Options 1 through 4 seem like a good solution for many churches. But experience tends to show that these approaches leave unexamined issues to move up the chain, where they surface later, on Church practice and leadership issues like whether gay Christians can serve as deacons or as ministers, or whether congregations can bless gay unions or marriages, or even whether gay couples can be photographed together for the church directory.

Option 5a strikes me—and many others, including many traditionalists—as incompatible with the way of Jesus, with the loving heartbeat of our congregations at their best, or with the evangelistic and discipling mission of the church. It feels more like how Jesus' adversaries acted, rather than like how he acted.

Option 5b assumes a traditionalist posture on the sexual ethics issue and places congregations and their leaders in the difficult position of enforcing it—across the entire life of the congregation, if they are to be consistent.

And the last one:

6. **The "normative reconsideration" option**. Some churches have studied the biblical texts and Christian tradition and contemporary realities and arrived at the conclusion that the heterosexual-only ethic needs to be revised.

That, of course, is the ultimate fork in the road.

CHAPTER 8

If This Is Where You Get Off the Bus

If this is where you get off the bus on this journey through the LGBT issue, here are seven things you and all of us can do.

IT SHOULD BE clear by now that the LGBT issue is by no means just one issue, and that its complexity requires a sufficiently complex response.

Careful readers will see that my approach in these chapters so far has been to try to identify areas of rather broad Christian agreement.

I hope that I have brought the vast majority of readers with me on the following claims, which I have generally identified as "forks in the road." None of them are directly related to the traditionalist/revisionist normative argument but they all impinge upon it.

- Whether rightly or not, the LGBT issue has become the hottest of hot-button issues in our generation, so ultimately *avoidism* proves insufficient. Everyone will have to figure out what they will think and do about this.

- Historic Christian understandings of sexuality are being reconsidered due to evidence offered in the lives of those who do not fit the historic heterosexual norm, together with associated research and mental health efforts. Some are open to this reconsideration, others fiercely opposed. The suffering of distressed LGBT Christians is a factor for most who are open to reconsidering Christian tradition.

- Several recent studies for the U.S. suggest a lesbian, gay, bisexual or transgender population ranging from 3.4 to 5 percent. Human sexual-orientation and sexual-identity diversity is a fact, seen all over the world.

- The admitted failure of the ex-gay movement and the great suffering it has caused has destroyed the plausibility of sexual-orientation-change efforts. Whatever pastoral approach the Church takes, it should not be that discredited and damaging one.

- Traditionalist Christians have come a long way since the 1970s in rejecting criminalization, discrimination, derogatory speech, bullying, violence, stigmatization and dehumanization of gay people. This is good news.

- While some traditionalist voices still dispute it, more are willing to acknowledge that the LGBT community contains a sizable population of professing Christians. Celibate gay Christians—sometimes called Side B Christians (see Chapter 4 for more on this)—are actually featured in much contemporary traditionalist literature.

- Churches have at least four options for welcoming gay seekers or Christians that do not involve rejection of heterosexual-only sexual ethics: these are the "ask no questions" option, the "who are we to judge?" option, the "dialogue for discernment/disputable matter" option, and the "pastoral accommodation" option. These implicate far broader questions in ecclesiology, such as what it means to be a church member, and whether churches will practice any form of what used to be called Church discipline. The LGBT issue surfaces, *but did not create*, this broader ecclesial issue.

There may be a large number of readers, perhaps especially traditionalists, who will want to get off the bus at this point. But if you do, I ask you to think a bit further about the implications of what you have "agreed to" so far. I think this leaves you—all of us—with a bit of homework that still needs to be done. Whether we decide to pursue this homework marks another major fork in the road.

1. *Read narratives of LGBT people, as well as reputable work in contemporary psychology* to inform your interactions with this population and the ways you speak privately and publicly about these issues. Dive in, if only to be better informed.

2. *Become aware that in any room with 20 or more people, the likelihood is that at least one is LGBT* in orientation and/ or identity. Add to this the friends and family members and others who fiercely love LGBT people. So any time you or I make any statement about "the gays" or "those people," we are likely speaking about people who are in the room with us. Speak with consequent care. People get their backs up when their loved ones are spoken of carelessly or contemptuously.

3. *Make a commitment never to accept derogatory speech or any form of bullying or mistreatment of LGBT people in your presence,* no more than you would allow people to use the N-word in your presence. If you are a parent or youth pastor, *never* allow kids to throw around terms like "gay" or "queer" as slurs. If you are a college student or teenager, *never* accept bullying or slurs without challenge. If your pastor says hurtful things from the pulpit, ask him or her to stop, and explain why. This commitment calls for courage, and a willingness to face scorn for standing up for gay people.

4. *Help parents respond in constructive ways when their
   children come out as gay or lesbian or express questions
   about their sexuality.* Make your church a context where
   parents *know* that the right response to their teenagers
   is *never* to reject them as human beings, never to throw
   them out. Did you know there are parents who tell their
   gay kids they wish those kids had never been born?
   Parents who refuse to acknowledge the existence of
   a child once he comes out as gay? Please: never, ever
   again! And if you know a teenager or young adult who
   has been rejected by their family because they are gay
   or lesbian, offer that child Christian love and hospitality.

5. *Get to know gay Christians (or ex-Christians) if you get the
   chance.* Listen to their stories with a teachable spirit.

6. *Become an advocate for the welcome of LGBT Christians
   in your congregation to the maximal point theologically
   possible in your setting.* Ask for some clarity from your
   church leaders. End avoidism.

7. *Even if you oppose civil gay marriage, consider public
   policy steps you can support.* Perhaps you can get
   behind anti-bullying curriculum in schools, or
   laws that classify physical attacks on gays as a hate
   crime. Perhaps you can support employment non-
   discrimination laws with appropriate exemptions for
   religious employers. Perhaps you can oppose often-
   demagogic legislation related to what the curriculum
   in public schools says about gay and lesbian people. In
   South Carolina, for example, teachers are permitted to
   mention homosexuality, but only in relation to sexually
   transmitted disease. (http://bit.ly/1vYmwbX). Whatever
   you decide that you can support, do so publicly. This
   sets a good example for others, and helps observers see
   that being Christian does not equal being anti-gay.

If this is where you get off the bus, please go with a new sense of resolve to love and serve LGBT people and to make your family, friendship group, and church a safe and loving place for everyone—and to resist the easier path of silence or indifference.

If you are willing to engage the issue further, read on as I tackle the normative dispute over same-sex relationships and the Bible.

CHAPTER 9

Biblical Inspiration, Human Interpretation

*About taking biblical inspiration and authority
seriously while humbly acknowledging a long history
of Christian fights over "what the Bible says."*

THE (PROTESTANT) BIBLE has 66 books, 1,189 chapters, and 31,273 verses, spoken, written, and edited over more than a millennium, in three different languages, in multiple social settings, by dozens of authors, with the last composition completed over 1,900 years ago. Despite these obvious evidences of human authorship, Christians in most confessions—I am one of them—also have historically claimed that this Bible is divinely inspired, truthful and trustworthy, carrying unique authority for guiding Christian belief and practice.

Protestants, more than other Christians, have tended to claim that the Bible is the primary or even the sole authority for determining truth in Christian theology and ethics. Some conservative Protestants have heightened their claims about the truth of Scripture with language such as *infallibility* and *inerrancy*. The more heightened and exclusive the claims about scriptural truth and authority, the more intense are the debates about how the Bible is to be interpreted. Claims about (my/our interpretation of) what "the Bible teaches" are viewed as settling all controverted issues.

Protestant traditionalists who stake their knowledge claims on biblical inspiration and authority—as opposed to Catholic traditionalists who more often stake such claims on natural law or the authority of divinely inspired Church teaching, of which the Bible was the first stage—generally express strong certainty that *the Bible* clearly teaches that there can be no morally legitimate same-sex (sexual-romantic) relationships. Some express incredulity that any alternative view is even under discussion. This is viewed as the ultimate open-and-shut case based on the "plain sense" of Scripture.

Skeptics, on the other hand, ask how exactly it is that Christians "know" that a particular portion of the (Protestant) Bible's 66 books, 1,189 chapters, and 31,273 verses should be selected and assembled for authoritative citation when it is time to argue about this or any other contemporary issue. They further ask how Christians know which way to interpret the verses they do select from the vast canon of Scripture.

I will ask you in upcoming chapters to consider how Christians *connect the biblical dots* within the vast canon of Scripture when it comes to this issue or any issue, and how we know who is doing it right. Who determines authoritatively whether we are connecting the biblical dots correctly?

Some skeptics consider this dot-connecting to be an essentially random, arbitrary and normless process, or one more determined by personal preference or power relations than anything else. (Some of those skeptics, by the way, are our own children, weary of our arguments.)

Sometimes such skepticism is well informed by knowledge of a long history of often bitter and sometimes deadly Christian argumentation about a wide range of theological and moral issues. In this history:

- Christians have come to fundamentally different conclusions about a myriad of issues.
- Christians have cited Scripture on all sides of such issues.

- Majority Christian opinion on various issues has sometimes shifted profoundly.
- Christians have often felt so passionate about Truth as they see it that they have sought to exclude or destroy their enemies, and have done so when sufficiently empowered.

Candidates for most bitterly contested theological and moral issues in 2,000 years of Christian history, issues about which determined Christians have quoted Scripture against each other, are plentiful. Random issues I've studied or witnessed that might make up such a list would include:

- Whether Catholics, or Protestants, or Baptists, or … should be persecuted or prosecuted.
- Whether Calvinism or Arminianism is more accurate in describing the divine and human roles in salvation.
- Whether charismatic/Pentecostal practices are mandatory, permissible, or "of the Devil."
- God's plan for men and women's roles in church, home and society.
- Whether torture of U.S. prisoners in the War on Terror might be morally legitimate.
- The morality of the sale and use of alcohol.
- The nature of proper Christian Sabbath observance.
- The morality of [name your] war.
- Whether slavery, colonization or abolition is mandated, permitted or banned by Scripture.
- The morality of continued U.S. racial segregation vs. racial integration in the 1950s and 1960s.
- God's preferred economic system between capitalism, socialism and a third way.
- Whether to cooperate with Nazism or stand in resistance, and at what points, in 1930s Germany.
- What to think and do about the Jews, theologically and politically.

- What to think about modern Israel.
- What eschatological (concerning death, judgment and the final destiny of the soul) scheme to embrace.
- The morality of apartheid in South Africa.
- The morality of child labor and other practices of unregulated industrial capitalism.
- Whether divorce might be permissible—and for what reasons.
- The morality of eating factory-farmed meat.
- [Your issue here]

With each one of these issues, it is easy to find relevant contemporaneous literature labeling the various sides as "*the* biblical position" and the opposing side as unbiblical.

The most interesting interlocutors in any contemporary Christian moral or theological debate are those aware that these oft-bloody historic interpretive battlegrounds fill the Christian landscape. These wise souls are therefore aware that *the texts of Scripture, on the one hand, and the interpretive process, on the other, are not the same thing.* They recognize that Christians fiercely committed to Christ, Scripture and truth, frequently do differ. They acknowledge that anyone's interpretation of a text or an issue at any given moment may turn out to be quite wrong. They understand therefore that humility and charity are called for when engaging in theological and moral argument. The least interesting debaters are those who seem to have learned nothing from our own conflicted history, and who therefore repeat that history over and over again in their certainty that *their reading of a text* is "God's own truth."

All of these fights over biblical texts and their interpretation, of course, lead many to a deep skepticism as to whether the canon of Scripture should be viewed as having such profound authority. Some of these skeptics are fellow Christians, often (ex-)Protestants scarred by too many battles over the Bible. Catholics and Eastern Orthodox, of course, have attempted to resolve their religious authority issues in different ways. You might have noticed that it's no easier for them. *Because humans see through a glass darkly, there is no way for us to avoid struggles over competing truth claims and how they are authoritatively grounded.*

Questions about why ancient sacred texts still carry so much authority in contemporary religious communities, or whether there is any rhyme or reason to how believers connect the biblical dots, or whether anyone can coherently claim to offer "the biblical perspective" on any issue, are exceedingly important. There are some who consider such questions so intrinsically devastating that all Christian efforts to propose a moral norm and ground it in biblical citations are essentially invalid—or that no one's perspective is any more defensible than anyone else's perspective. How often I have quoted a Bible passage in an online article about something and immediately been met by derisive citations of Leviticus. Whimsical humor about the folly of attempting to read the Bible as if it might be taken as authoritative is common today.

In these chapters, I am not really writing for such skeptics. I am instead writing for fellow believers who, despite it all, have retained strong belief in the inspiration and authority of the Bible for the Christian life, as I have.

I am writing for Christians who believe that there are indeed better and worse, more or less defensible ways of selecting, interpreting and applying sacred Scriptures to address specific issues.

I am writing for those who believe that anyone attempting to propose moral norms for contemporary Christians needs to do their biblical homework, show that work (like in algebra class) and test it in community.

I also am writing for those who are aware that while theological and moral inquiry rely on excellent biblical exegesis and interpretation, *broader processes of analysis and discernment, in loving Christian community, integrating head and heart, are required to understand not just what a text once meant, but what it means for the believing Church today.*

I write for those who think that honest, fair-minded individual and collective inquiry is indispensable in Christian life, and that this is in fact how truth is sought among us, with the aid of the Holy Spirit.

Next, in this spirit, I will begin digging into the texts most relevant to the LGBT issue.

CHAPTER 10

How Traditionalists Connect the Biblical Dots

How traditionalists on the LGBT issue "connect the biblical dots," and how not to argue against them.

THE ESSENTIALS OF the traditionalist reading of scripture on same-sex relationships can be rendered by this formula, though of course there are variations:

> *Genesis 1-2 + Genesis 19 + Leviticus 18:22/20:13 + Judges 19 + Matthew 19:1-12/Mark 10:2-12 + Romans 1:26-27 + 1 Corinthians 6:9/1 Timothy 1:10 [+ Ephesians 5:22-33 and all other biblical references to sex and marriage assuming or depicting male + female] = a clear biblical ban on same-sex relationships.*

Here I summarize these references in as balanced a manner as I can:

Genesis 1-2 offers creation accounts in which 1) God makes humanity male and female and commands/blesses them to be fruitful and multiply and 2) God responds to the man's loneliness by creating woman, then giving her to the man, with the narrator connecting this to marriage.

Genesis 19 and Judges 19 both tell stories of perverse local city men seeking to sexually assault male guests receiving hospitality in local households.

Leviticus 18:22 commands men not to lie with men as with women; Leviticus 20:13 prescribes the death penalty for this offense. The Hebrew word *toevah* used in these passages has generally been translated as "abomination."

Matthew 19:1-12/Mark 10:2-12 are the main texts depicting Jesus responding to questions about the morality of men divorcing their wives. He appeals to the two creation texts noted above to ground his rigorous response, setting strict limits on initiating divorce. A teaching about eunuchs is appended to the end of Matthew's version.

Romans 1:26-27 is part of an argument Paul is making about why everyone needs the salvation offered in Jesus Christ. Possibly in an effort to illustrate the idolatry and sinfulness of the Gentile part of the human community, Paul apparently makes negative reference to same-sex sexual acts on the part of both men and women. Later, he lists 21 further illustrations.

1 Corinthians 6:9 and 1 Timothy 1:10 both offer vice lists as part of moral exhortations to Christian living. The Greek words *malakoi* and especially Paul's neologism *arsenokoitai*, used in these passages, have sometimes been translated into English as "homosexuals" (*New American Standard Bible*) or "sodomites" (*New Revised Standard Version*). These translations, though they vary widely in many English Bibles, have been formative for many Christians.

Other texts in which it is solely men and women having sex, and men and women marrying, could also be and sometimes are listed on the traditionalist side.

If we take the most commonly cited texts on the issue from the traditionalist side, they are derived from 11 of the 1,189 chapters in the Bible. But it is not unusual to hear the broader claim that whenever the Bible mentions licit sex, it is exclusively heterosexual.

∾

In future chapters, I will seek to address at least briefly the substantive interpretive issues around each of the major passages, and propose other possible ways of connecting the biblical dots.

But for now, I want to make a few recommendations about how *not* to argue against traditionalists. These claims are made on theological, ethical and prudential grounds, and are directed mainly at my progressive friends. Please, friends:

Do not dismiss the traditionalist-cited passages as "clobber verses," deployed with malice in order to harm gay people. Certainly there are some who use the Bible in egregious ways to clobber others, but also remember the good-hearted Christian folks who are simply trying to be faithful Christians and aren't clobbering anyone when they cite the passages they think are most relevant to the issue.

Do not dismiss whole authors (Paul) or sections (Old Testament) of scripture as if we good, contemporary folks know that they have little to say to our enlightened modern world, at least not if you want to be taken seriously by traditional Christians.

Do not dismiss people who cite the Bible against your view simply as fundamentalists or some other derogatory phrase. It's not helpful, and most of the time it's not fair. Name-calling rarely advances the search for truth or the health of Christian community.

Do not dismiss traditionalist Christian sexual ethics as simply part of an overall anti-body, anti-sex, anti-woman, anti-pleasure agenda. Surely this has been a strand of Christian history. But I can point you to a zillion Christians who love bodies, sex, women, men and pleasure, but read the Bible in a traditionalist way on this issue.

Do not simply point to broad themes of liberation, justice or inclusion of the marginalized as if those important biblical imperatives *ipso facto* invalidate the need to deal with the texts cited on the traditionalist side.

Do not assume that the issue is settled by making claims to being "prophetic." This is a big claim, and it helps to remember that some on the other side of this issue are also making it. Only God can validate who is really being prophetic.

Do not just say that it's time for Christians to "catch up with the culture" or stop falling "behind the times." The fact that a particular culture has moved to a particular point does not prove anything, because cultures are sometimes quite wrong.

The argument over sexuality today is a serious one. It requires serious work. But when progressives default to these responses and refuse to engage the real concerns of the other side, they come across as *fundamentally unserious about Scripture—or theology—or ethics—or Christian discipleship*. And I suspect that this is one primary reason for the level of passion about this issue on the traditionalist side. They consider the LGBT issue a symbol of a far broader problem in the life of the church. That concern, too, must be addressed.

CHAPTER 11

The Sins of Sodom (and Gibeah)

An interpretation of the Sodom (and Gibeah) stories, so fatefully destructive in forming historic Christian attitudes on the LGBT issue.

TRADITIONALIST CHRISTIANS ARGUE that there can be no legitimate same-sex relationships because they are banned by the Bible. Thus, even where traditionalists acknowledge the existence of enduring same-sex orientation, they enjoin lifetime celibacy for gay and lesbian Christians. Revisionist Christians who adhere otherwise to a traditionalist sexual ethic suggest that a covenantal, monogamous same-sex relationship should be considered permissible for gay Christians.

In the last chapter, I said that the traditionalist position is grounded in a pattern of connecting the biblical dots that looks like this:

Genesis 1-2 + Genesis 19 + Leviticus 18:22/20:13 + Judges 19 + Matthew 19:1-12/Mark 10:2-12 + Romans 1:26-27 + 1 Corinthians 6:9/1 Timothy 1:10 [+ all biblical references to sex and marriage assuming or depicting male + female] = a clear biblical ban on same-sex relationships.

In the next several chapters I want to look at the most important issues raised by examining these texts, and especially consider the relative merits of traditionalist and alternative interpretations.

Let's begin by tackling the Genesis 19/Judges 19 pair, and related echoes in Scripture. The two stories are remarkably similar. Both involve gangs of men wanting to violate visitors being sheltered in a local household in accord with ancient Near Eastern hospitality standards. Both involve the offer of women as an alternative to the baying crowds. In Genesis 19 the women (daughters) are refused, while in Judges 19 the woman (a concubine, who is also a guest, but not protected) is accepted by the gang, tortured and raped either to death or nearly to death, and then dismembered later by her own master. According to Gerhard von Rad, these texts probably have at least a "distant dependence" on each other.[12]

Both are "texts of terror," as Phyllis Trible so devastatingly called them—among the most disturbing in Scripture.[13]

I will focus on the Sodom and Gomorrah story because of its far greater impact in the rest of Scripture and Christian tradition and its role in the LGBT discussion.

The broader outlines of the story are familiar to most readers of Scripture. It stretches at least from Genesis 18:16-19:38, though the first reference to Sodom and Gomorrah is in 10:19. Historical-critical biblical scholars are convinced that several narrative strands are edited together here. As the text stands in final form, it is in part an etiological (explaining causes or origins of something) story meant to explain the catastrophe that wiped out the cities that once existed on the plain near the Dead Sea (compare with: 19:24-25). In part it's a story about the contrast between the character of a holy God and wayward humanity at its worst. Its most interesting dimension,

---

12 Gerhard von Rad, *Genesis:* (Old Testament Library), revised edition (Philadelphia: Westminster Press, 1972), p. 218.
13 Phyllis Trible, *Texts of Terror: Literary-Feminist Readings of Biblical Narratives* (Philadelphia: Fortress Press 1984), ch. 3.

as Walter Brueggemann emphasizes in his commentary on Genesis, is in the revelatory power of the story of Abraham negotiating with God to save these cities from destruction. Here we see the extraordinary role that Abraham is beginning to play as covenant and dialogue partner with God, embodiment of justice and righteousness, and bearer of blessing to humanity. There are notes of grace here that point to Jesus and the Gospel.[14]

Abraham asks that if only 50, 40, 30, 20 or 10 righteous people are found in these wicked cities, will not the God of justice spare Sodom? (18:22-33). God repeatedly says yes. Divine retribution on the many will be withheld due to the righteousness of the few.

But when they get to Sodom, the two emissary-angels do not find even 10 righteous. Abraham's nephew Lot, who lives in Sodom, offers exemplary hospitality to the two "men." But late at night "the men of the city" surround and attack Lot's house en masse. They want to "know" the visitors whom Lot is sheltering. Lot refuses, leaving the safety of his house to beg the crowd to relent, and even offering his virgin daughters to appease the crowd. But the men refuse, saying, "Stand back! This fellow came here as an alien, and he would play the judge! Now we will deal worse with you than with them" (Genesis 19:9). Their attack is repelled only with miraculous angelic help. Sodom and Gomorrah are incinerated the next day, after Lot's family is led away by the angels to safety.

It was once common to interpret this story as a clear indictment on "homosexuality." Fatefully, of course, the term "sodomy" is derived from this story (a term introduced in the 11th century, according to Mark Jordan).[15]

---

14 Walter Brueggemann, *Genesis: Interpretation: A Bible Commentary for Teaching and Preaching* (Atlanta: John Knox Press, 1982), pp. 162-177.

15 Mark D. Jordan, *The Invention of Sodomy in Christian Theology* (Chicago: University of Chicago Press, 1997).

The cultural impact of both the story and the term have been enormous. But now few serious biblical interpreters think this story is about homosexuality at all. It has certainly receded in the traditionalist argument.

We know before Chapter 19 starts that Sodom and Gomorrah are legendarily sinful towns, though we don't know why. But after the harrowing attack on Lot and his visitors, the reader now knows quite a bit about the nature of that sinfulness. This is a horrifying tale about the attempted gang rape of strangers, the shocking violation of Israelite and ancient Near Eastern standards of hospitality, Lot's willingness to sacrifice his own daughters to the crowd, and the depravity of an entire city—all exacerbated by the fact that the intended targets happen to be angelic emissaries of a holy God. The story is filled with violence and the threat of harm. Notice that when Lot protects his guests, his "brothers" expand their threat to Lot himself: "We will deal worse with you than with them." The parallel story in Judges 20:5 makes absolutely clear that it was violence the men wanted, including sexual violence, and violence they inflicted.

Sodom and Gomorrah, their sin and God's punishment, became resonant symbols. When cited within the rest of Scripture, even the names of these towns became a byword for total human evil and devastating divine judgment (Deuteronomy 29:23, 32:32; Isaiah 1:9f, 3:9, 13:19; Jeremiah 23:14, 49:18, 50:40; Lamentations 4:6; Ezekiel 16:46-50; Amos 4:11; Zephaniah 2:9; Matthew 10:15/Luke 10:10-12, Romans 9:29, 2 Peter 2:6-10, Jude 6-7; compare with: Psalms 11:6). The starkest way to warn Israel or the Church of impending judgment was to drop in a Sodom reference.

But never once in these intra-biblical references to Sodom is their evil described as same-sex interest or behavior. In Isaiah 1:9-23, a host of sins are named but mainly related to abuses of public justice. In Jeremiah 23:14 it's adultery, lying and unwillingness to repent. Ezekiel 16:49 describes their sins as pride, excess food, prosperous ease and lack of care for the poor. In Amos and Zephaniah the issues are pride, mocking and oppressing the poor. Inter-testamental works of Sirach (16:8), 3 Maccabees (2:5), and Wisdom (19:15) still talk about Sodom and Gomorrah, and still don't connect their sin to sexuality at all.

The only biblical references to Sodom with any *possible* suggestion of same-sex behavior are Jude 6-8 and the parallel text in 2 Peter 2:6-7, with their references to unholy interest in "other flesh" (Jude 7). In the context of an interpretation of Genesis 19 that was already convinced the story is about same-sex behavior, these two late New Testament texts were read as confirmation. But look closely. They represent fragments of tradition referring to unholy human interest in *sex with angels*, a theme derived from the book of Enoch, with reference back to the mysterious Genesis 6 story about angels who had sex with human women.

The most illuminating comparison to the Sodom and Gomorrah story is to wartime or prison rape. Think about how one of the first images that comes to mind when thinking about prisons is the fear of getting raped there.

The men of Sodom want gang rape. They are more interested in men than in Lot's daughters because in a patriarchal society men held greater worth, and thus their violation was viewed as a greater offense than violating a woman.[16]

I would also suggest that the men wanted to dominate, humiliate and harm the male visitors precisely *by treating them like defenseless women*. In sexist social systems, the most outrageous thing you can do to a man is to treat him like a woman. The Sodom story is about the attempted gang rape of men, because they are strangers, because they are vulnerable, and because they are a juicy target for humiliation and violation. It is about a town that had sunk to the level of the most depraved battlefield or prison.

---

16 William Loader, *The New Testament on Sexuality* (Grand Rapids: William B. Eerdmans Publishing Company, 2012), p. 29.

Genesis 19 and Judges 19 are narratives with huge implications for the ethics of war, prison, gender, violence and rape. But they have nothing to do with the morality of loving, covenantal same-sex relationships.

CHAPTER 12

Leviticus, Abomination and Jesus

Two texts in Leviticus, and complexities related to what Christians are to make of them today.

ALMOST NO CHRISTIAN ever quotes the Old Testament book of Leviticus today, a text which mainly, though not exclusively, contains worship instructions rendered obsolete for Jews themselves centuries ago by the destruction of the last Jewish Temple. However, two texts plucked from Leviticus are regularly cited by Christians in the LGBT debate:

> *You shall not lie with a male as with a woman; it is an abomination.*
>
> **—Leviticus 18:22**

> *If a man lies with a male as with a woman, both of them have committed an abomination; they shall be put to death; their blood is upon them.*
>
> **—Leviticus 20:13**

Variations of the Hebrew term *toevah* (usually translated "detestable" as an adjective or "abomination" as a noun, as here) are used 117 times in the Old Testament, led especially by Deuteronomy, Ezekiel and Proverbs. The term refers to practices abhorred by God and thus by God's law and God's prophets.

In Leviticus 18 and 20, all kinds of sexual acts are banned and collectively called abominations, including sex with blood relatives and within a broader family circle and sex with a menstruating woman.

Food is often connected with the concept: Deuteronomy names eating pork, rabbit, shellfish and animals that are already dead as abominations (14:3-21).

For Ezekiel, abomination is a central term to describe all of the various offenses of Israel that have incurred the fierce judgment of the Lord:

- Ezekiel 18:10-13 names violence, eating upon the mountains (probably idol-worship), adultery, oppressing the poor and needy, robbery, not restoring one's pledge, lifting up eyes to idols and charging interest on loans as abominations worthy of death.
- Ezekiel 22:6-12 adds contemptuous treatment of parents, extortion of aliens, mistreatment of orphans and widows, profaning of Sabbaths, slandering and taking bribery to shed blood and various sexual sins (though not naming same-sex relations) as abominations.
- Ezekiel 44:5-7 describes as abominations admitting foreigners to the temple and profaning the temple when offering sacrifices of fat and blood.

Proverbs names the following as abominations: the perverse (3:32); haughty eyes, a lying tongue, hands that shed innocent blood, a heart that devises wicked plans, feet that hurry to run to evil, a lying witness who testifies falsely, one who sows discord in a family (6:15-17); untruthful speech (8:7); crooked minds (11:20); false balances and scales used in business (11:1, 20:10, 20:23); lying lips (12:22); the sacrifice of the wicked (15:8, 21:27); evil plans (15:26); arrogance (16:5); kings doing evil (16:12); justifying the wicked/condemning the righteous (17:15); the scoffer (24:9); not listening to the law (28:9); and the unjust (29:27).

It is relevant to note that never again outside of Leviticus are same-sex acts mentioned in Old Testament law, leaving at least 111 of the 117 uses of the term "abomination" to describe other issues. It is interesting how few of those other acts or character qualities are ever described as abominations by Christians today.

∼

A critical question directly relevant to our topic is what exactly it was about male same-sex intercourse that triggered the abomination charge found in these two verses. There is no scholarly agreement, though one interpretation is especially important.

Some, such as Gordon Wenham, have noted its placement in Leviticus 18 after an introduction calling Israel to be set apart from the practices of its Canaanite and Egyptian neighbors.[17]

The issue may then be preserving Israel's clear differentiation from its pagan neighbors, especially their idolatrous practices and perhaps also cultic prostitution.[18]

Old Testament scholar Phyllis Bird goes further to argue that *toevah* "is not an ethical term, but a term of boundary marking."[19]

---

17 Gordon J. Wenham, *Leviticus: New International Commentary on the Old Testament* (Grand Rapids: William B. Eerdmans Publishing Company, 1979), pp. 250-252.

18 James V. Brownson, *Bible, Gender, Sexuality: Reframing the Church's Debate on Same-Sex Relationships* (Grand Rapids: William B. Eerdmans Publishing Company, 2013), p. 270.

19 Phyllis A. Bird, "The Bible in Christian Ethical Deliberation Concerning Homosexuality: Old Testament Contributions," in *Homosexuality, Science, and the "Plain Sense" of Scripture*, ed. David L. Balch (Grand Rapids, MI: William B. Eerdmans Publishing Company, 2000), p. 152.

That may be a bit too strong, but it does point to the fact that cultural practices, especially related to bodily matters, and often grounded in religious tradition, set peoples apart from one another and frequently evoke mutual disgust when differences are encountered at close range.

Jewish biblical scholar and Conservative rabbi Jacob Milgrom notes the lack of any reference to female same-sex relations in Leviticus 18/20. He suggests that it was the male "spilling of the seed" (compare with: the Onan story in Genesis 38), thus the symbolic loss or waste of life, that was the primary motivation for this law. Scholars generally agree that uneasiness about non-procreative sexuality was a factor in Old Testament and perhaps also New Testament treatments of same-sex issues. Milgrom also notes that Leviticus 18 is addressed to Israelites residing in the Holy Land, and no one else, suggesting a very narrow range of applicability either then or now.[20]

Biblical scholars Richard Elliott Friedman and Shawna Dolansky have zeroed in on the gender dimension, suggesting that "such intercourse would necessarily denigrate the passive partner and violate his equal status under God's law."[21]

Bible, Gender, Sexuality Which means: The penetrated recipient allows himself to be treated like a woman, which is itself the abomination because of its profound violation of hierarchical, male-dominant gender roles. But if this is the reason for the ban, it raises questions for any Christian who does not share beliefs in the lesser worth and dignity of women.

In her famous work *Purity and Danger*, Mary Douglas suggested that the categories of holy/unholy and clean/unclean

---

20 Jacob Milgrom, *Leviticus: A Continental Commentary* (Minneapolis: Fortress Press, 2004), pp. 196-197.

21 Richard Elliott Friedman and Shawna Dolansky, *The Bible Now* (Oxford: Oxford University Press, 2011), p. 35. Brownson, *Bible, Gender, Sexuality*, agrees that male honor was a significat factor. See p. 272.

in Leviticus are rooted in understandings of wholeness, completeness and right order. The sexual morality injunctions of Leviticus 18/20, then, have to do with "keeping distinct the categories of creation."[22]

Robert Gagnon, probably the leading scholarly traditionalist Christian voice, also argues for this view, in part by linking the final version of Leviticus to Genesis as part of the Pentateuch (the Torah). He sees a consistent biblical rejection of same-sex relations based on God's design in creation.[23]

It will become clear during the course of these chapters that claims from the moral order established by God in creation are extremely important in the Christian discussion of the LGBT issue.

~

Leviticus 20:13 commands the death penalty. If Old Testament laws enjoining the death penalty are to be taken as authoritative today for Christians, as some suggest by citing Leviticus 20:13, it seems appropriate to list here other passages that demand death for various wrongs:

Offenses punishable by the death penalty in the Holiness Code of Leviticus: child sacrifice (Leviticus 20:2); cursing parents (20:9); various sexual acts, primarily incestuous or within the family circle (20:11-15); being a medium or wizard (20:27); blaspheming the name of the Lord (24:17); and murder (24:21); also, persons placed under the ban (devoted to destruction in holy war) must be killed, never ransomed (27:29).

---

22 Mary Douglas, *Purity and Danger: An Analysis of Concepts of Pollution and Taboo* (London: Routledge Classics, 2002), p. 67. More recently, James Brownson essentially agrees, while updating the analysis: James V. Brownson, *Bible, Gender, Sexuality: Reframing the Church's Debate on Same-Sex Relationships* (Grand Rapids: William B. Eerdmans Publishing Company, 2013), p. 269.

23 Robert Gagnon, *The Bible and Homosexual Practice: Texts and Hermeneutics* (Nashville: Abingdon Press, 2001), p. 141.

Other offenses punishable by death in Old Testament law: touching Mt. Sinai while God is giving the law (Exodus 21:12); striking a person mortally (21:15); striking father or mother (21:16); kidnapping (21:17); cursing a parent (21:29); failure to restrain a violent animal (22:19); bestiality (31:14); Sabbath breaking (31:15, 35:2; compare with: Numbers 15:35); anyone other than a Levite coming near the tabernacle (Numbers 3:10); anyone other than Moses, Aaron, or Aaron's sons camping in front of the tabernacle to the east (Numbers 3:38); an outsider coming near the altar area (Numbers 18:7); and, striking another with an object so that the other dies (Numbers 35:16-21) in which case only the "avenger of blood" shall execute the sentence (Numbers 35:21, 30-34; compare with: Deuteronomy 19:11-13). Deuteronomy adds the death penalty for divining by dreams to lead Israel to idolatry (13:1-5) and enticement to idol worship, even by a family member (13:6-11); a town that goes astray to worship idols is to be destroyed utterly, including its livestock (13:12-18), as in other holy war situations (Deuteronomy 7, Joshua 2,8,10, etc.). Children who disobeyed their parents were also to be executed (Deuteronomy 21:18-21).

Various ritual offenses by the priests described as incurring guilt and bringing death: failure to wear the properly designed priestly robes, turban and undergarments into and out of the holy place (Exodus 28:31-43); failure to wash hands and feet before entering the tabernacle or the altar (Exodus 30:17-21); failure to stay the full seven days of the priestly consecration rite (Leviticus 8:33-35); drinking wine or strong drink when entering the tabernacle (Leviticus 10:8-9); failure to make proper ritual cleansing after sexual emissions and discharges of blood (Leviticus 15); failure to prepare properly before entering the tabernacle on the Day of Atonement (Leviticus 16); and violations of bodily cleanness regulations by a priest entering the tabernacle (Leviticus 22:1-9).

Do Christians quoting Leviticus 20:13 support the death penalty for those committing same-sex acts? If not, why not?

If so, do they support the death penalty for all of the offenses listed in the previous three paragraphs?

~

I review these Old Testament legal materials in order to ask Christians who quote selectively from such materials to *describe and defend their principle of selection, interpretation, and application.* In other words, unless one accepts every Old Testament legal text as authoritative for Christians today in the exact manner in which it is written, what alternative hermeneutical (a method of interpreting the Bible) principle is to be employed?

The issue is actually quite complex, and has challenged serious readers of the Bible for all of Christian history.

It is not as simple as saying that *Christians accept all the laws offered in the Old Testament, just not the death penalty statutes that go with them*—because very, very few if any Christians accept all the laws themselves, such as those requiring genocidal violence against idolatrous towns or the adherence to kosher food regulations or the priestly sacrifice rules.

It is also not as simple as saying that *Christians accept the moral laws offered in the Old Testament, just not the ceremonial, cultic, dietary, or civil laws*—because, as Old Testament scholar Martin Noth wrote, "Here in the Old Testament ... there is no question of different categories of commandment, but only of the Will of God binding on Israel, revealed in a great variety of concrete requirements."[24]

Any differentiation of authority in terms of categories of Old Testament legal materials is foreign to the materials themselves. And no clear delineation along these lines is offered in the New Testament.

It is also not as simple as saying *Christians may not accept all the laws offered in the Old Testament, but we do seek to*

---

24 Martin Noth, *Leviticus: Old Testament Library* (Philadelphia: Westminster Press, 1965), p. 16.

practice the principles behind them, as Gordon Wenham, among others, has suggested.[25]

While this move is often compelling, other times the principles are not clear, and still other times they are clear but we cannot accept them as Christians. Consider the principle of collective responsibility and therefore collective punishment of the entire population of a town for its prevailing religious practices, or the principle that the "unclean" (like menstruating women) should be excluded from community.

If we say that *Christians may not accept all the laws or the principles offered in the Old Testament, but we are committed to belief in the core character of God as revealed there, such as the idea that God is holy and demands holiness,* this is better. But this does not resolve the question of whether all same-sex relationships violate the character of a holy God.

Nor does it settle the question of whether divine holiness—at least the kind of holiness emphasized in Leviticus—fits with the character of God as taught and embodied by Jesus Christ. It is impossible to treat any question related to the applicability of an Old Testament legal text for Christians without considering the person and work of Jesus Christ, as well as the way he handled Old Testament law. Here it is relevant to say that terms related to *toevah* are very rare in the New Testament, used only in a few passages, two of them in Revelation (Luke 16:15, Revelation 17:4-5, 21:27; compare with: Matthew 24:15). This widely attested Old Testament term played little role in Jesus' vocabulary, and it is easier to argue that he challenged this way of understanding God's character than that he reinforced it.

On the other extreme, it is too simple to just say that *the entirely of Old Testament law has been set aside for Christians.* It is certainly the case that Old Testament law goes through a considerable sifting process in the hands of Jesus and his followers. The Apostle Paul was the most famous sifter of them all, as is evidenced by constant references in his letters. He was aided by a pretty key assist from Peter (Acts 10). Acts 15

25 Wenham, *Leviticus,* pp. 32-33.

offers a famous account of one particular compromise solution. The entire book of Hebrews constitutes a highly complex reflection on the matter of how Jewish Law and Jesus Christ relate to each other, using an old/new, worse/better paradigm with problematic implications for 2,000 years of Jewish-Christian relations. But where Old Testament laws are reaffirmed in the New Testament, as some say happens with these Levitical texts, then the case for their continued authority increases dramatically.

It is a fair summary to say that once Jesus comes along, and the Church is founded, neither 2,000 years ago nor today has it been as simple as just quoting a passage from Leviticus to settle a matter of Christian morality.

It should be noted that the Jewish tradition itself has never simply read Hebrew Bible texts at face value, but instead considered them through a highly sophisticated mediating body of rabbinic tradition, questioning and argumentation. It is really pretty scandalous how Christians extract ancient texts of the Hebrew Bible, call it our Old Testament, and then interpret them without any reference to the way Jewish biblical interpretation itself has proceeded for over two millennia.

So: The two sentences in Leviticus 18:22 and 20:13 are duly noted. They rightly figure in the Church's moral deliberation, with appropriate caveats suggested here. They do not resolve the LGBT issue.

CHAPTER 13

Two Odd Little Words

*Two obscure Greek words whose uncertain translation
renders use of them for the LGBT issue problematic.*

IN FALL 2014, I wrote a letter to my ethics survey class
here at McAfee School of Theology. One line read: "Thanks
for the name-hugs."

Imagine a scholar studying the writings of Gushee 2,000
years from now for a new Nepalese translation and commentary. (Humor me here.) This scholar has only a reading
knowledge of English, and only a limited understanding of
21st century American culture. She stumbles upon this phrase
"name-hugs." She does not know what it means. She reads the
entire email for context clues. She examines all my correspondence, and then all my other published writings. She searches
a database of phrases in 21st century Christian theology and
ethics. She broadens her quest to cover all known 21st century
American English phrases. In the last database she reads that
"hug" generally meant: "A form of physical intimacy in which
two people put their arms around the neck, back, or waist of
one another and hold each other closely." There is a corre-
sponding word for hug in 41st century Nepalese so this is a
good start.

But what of this phrase name-hug? She turns to images. A
search of photos and drawings associated with the phrase

name-hugs in global culture is inconclusive, though images of
a snowman named Olaf come up first. Further searches reveal
that he was a character in the animated movie *Frozen*. Our
scholar tentatively concludes that Gushee probably meant to
say thank you to his students for providing him with images of
Olaf the snowman. But if she is a careful scholar she will write
a footnote acknowledging that his meaning cannot be determined conclusively.

There are only 42 people in the world who until now knew
what I meant by that phrase name-hugs—the recipients of
my email. I now resolve the mystery: I made up the phrase to
describe a new name-learning technique. I read off of index
cards that each student had given me the names of those few
students whose faces I could not identify yet. I then asked
each person whose name I was uncertain about to come forward and give me a (brief, public, sisterly/brotherly) hug while
I called each by his or her name. I thought that this would
help me break through the anonymity of a large class. Name-
hugs. And it worked!

~

In 1 Corinthians 6:9 and 1 Timothy 1:10, Paul (in the second case, probably a pseudonymous "Paul") deploys two "vice
lists"—a common enough rhetorical strategy in the Greco-Roman world—to communicate to his readers condemnation of
sinful behavior. With regard to 1 Corinthians, most scholars
agree that Paul is dealing with an especially unruly congregation, some of whom have fallen prey to moral laxity, including
in sexuality. Paul writes to correct that, and to make it per-
fectly clear that the salvation offered by grace does not also
offer an exemption from basic moral requirements. Then follow 10 types of people who, Paul warns, will not "inherit the
kingdom of God." In 1 Timothy 1, the context for the vice list
is more obscure. It falls under a discussion of "the law," and
the author's concern about false teachers apparently focusing overmuch on the law. Paul says that the law is mainly

intended for the godless. Then follow seven examples of such godlessness.

In both vice lists the Greek word *arsenokoitai* is used. In the first list, the word *malakoi* is directly in front of it. A vast, highly contested scholarly literature exists to parse out the meaning of these two odd little words.

Consider *malakoi*. This is a Greek word whose English translations range wildly from "weakling" to "wanton" to "debauchers" to "licentious" to "sensual" to "effeminate" to "male prostitutes" to a composite of *malakoi* plus *arsenokoitai* translating them together as "men who have sex with men" or "homosexuals." The word literally means "soft" and is used elsewhere in the New Testament *only* to describe the soft or fine clothing worn by those who are rich (Matthew 11:8/Luke 7:25).

William Loader says the word does basically mean soft, and if applied to a man would be a pejorative attack on his masculinity.[26]

Dale Martin finds that the meaning could be extended to mock men who allowed themselves to be treated like women sexually—to be penetrated, though a wide variety of other terms were more commonly used, leading him to doubt whether that meaning should be assumed in this case. He instead focuses on a broader semantic range related to soft, such as self-indulgent, sexually undisciplined, luxurious living.[27]

On the other end of the spectrum, Robert Gagnon reads the term to apply precisely to the passive partner in male

---

26 William Loader, *The New Testament on Sexuality* (Grand Rapids: William B. Eerdmans Publishing Company, 2012), p. 327.
27 Dale Martin, *Sex and the Single Savior: Gender and Sexuality in Biblical Interpretation* (Louisville: Westminster John Knox, 2006), pp. 37-50.

same-sex relations (penetrated men), and not just to "male prostitutes," as in the New International Version.[28]

But William Loader again points out that if Paul wanted to say precisely that he had other terms available to him.[29]

Got it figured out yet?

As for *arsenokoitai*, the only two times the word appears in the New Testament are found in 1 Corinthians 6:9 and 1 Timothy 1:10, and most scholars believe Paul coined the phrase. It appears only very rarely in ancient Greek writings after Paul, mostly also in vice lists. Like my new phrase name-hug, the word *arsenokoitai* (plural for *arsenokoites*) is a composite word, made up from two previously existing words that do not seem to have been put together before in Greek literature.

A significant number of scholars, such as Richard Hays, think Paul is not being altogether original, but instead alluding here to the Septuagint (Greek) translation of the Hebrew Bible's Leviticus 18:22 and 20:13.[30]

Or perhaps, suggests Anthony Thiselton, if Paul is not directly alluding to those texts, he is at least pointing to traditional Jewish sexual ethics—which he wanted now to teach as Christian sexual ethics.[31]

In the Septuagint (a Greek version of the Old Testament), both Leviticus 18:22 and 20:13 contain the terms *arsenos* and *koiten*. Leviticus 20:13 is more important here because it puts

28 Robert Gagnon, *Homosexuality and the Bible: Two Views* (Minneapolis: Fortress Press, 2009), pp. 82-83.

29 Loader, *New Testament on Sexuality*, pp. 328-329.

30 New Testament scholar Richard Hays essentially takes this position, though using the term "evidently" as a qualifier. See Richard B. Hays, *First Corinthians: Interpretation Bible Commentary* (Louisville: John Knox Press, 1997), p. 97.

31 This is essentially the position taken by Anthony C. Thiselton, who also offers an indispensably thorough review of the state of the scholarship. Thiselton, *The First Epistle to the Corinthians: New International Greek Testament Commentary* (Grand Rapids, MI/ Cambridge: William B. Eerdmans Publishing Company, 2000), pp. 438-453.

the terms directly together. Many scholars find that linguistic parallel or connection conclusive evidence as to Paul's source and meaning, even though there is no evidence it had ever been done before.

As Marti Nissinen summarizes the overall scholarly conversation: "These attempts … show how difficult it really is to determine the actual meaning of this word in different contexts."[32]

But because there is an English-language Christian community, the Greek New Testament does indeed need to get translated into English, and translators have to come up with some kind of word for *arsenokoitai*.

Here are examples of how the word *arsenokoitai* has been translated into English over 425 years, with appreciation to Matthew Vines for this compilation:

- Geneva Bible (1587): "buggerers"
- King James Bible (1607): "abusers of themselves with mankind"
- Mace New Testament (1729): "the brutal"
- Wesley's New Testament (1755): "sodomites"
- Douay-Rheims (1899): "liers with mankind"
- Revised Standard Version (1946): "homosexuals"
- Phillips Bible (1958): "pervert"
- Today's English Version (1966): "homosexual perverts"
- New International Version (1973): "homosexual offenders"
- New American Bible (1987): "practicing homosexuals"

Working from most English interpretations/translations of a Pauline neologism (a new word Paul had coined), most English-reading Christians and most English-speaking preachers have naturally concluded that Paul is condemning either/both all homosexual people or all people who perform same-sex acts. (Sometimes in harshly derogatory terms, such

32 Marti Nissinen, *Homoeroticism in the Biblical World: A Historical Perspective* (Minneapolis: Fortress Press Press, 1998), p. 117.

as in the unforgivable *Today's English Version* and Phillips
translations.) Some have also concluded from 1 Corinthians
6:9 that all such people are simply excluded from heaven—i.e.,
heading straight to hell. This is despite other New Testament texts related to the criteria for eternal life, such as those
emphasizing God's grace for forgiven but imperfect sinners
who believe (consider John 3:16). And few who cite 1 Corinthians 6:9 to say that "practicing" gays are going to hell also
say that "practicing" greedy people or drunkards are going to
hell.

Most English-speaking Christians would have no idea that
arsenokoitai was a new word that Paul possibly coined whose
meaning and translation are contested.

They would not know of the intense debate among classics
scholars and New Testament interpreters as to what Paul was
thinking about when he was (apparently or clearly) talking
about same-sex activity in the Greco-Roman world. Consensual adult sex? Man-boy sex/abuse? Prostitution? Rape? Abuse
of slaves? They would not, for example, have read Michael
Vasey's observation that in imperial Rome same-sex activity
was "strongly associated with idolatry, slavery, and social dominance ... often the assertion of the strong over the bodies of
the weak."[33]

Is that what we think today when we hear the term
"homosexual"?

They would not know of the claim of New Testament
scholar Dale Martin that of the few uses of the term *arsenokoites* in Greek literature outside of the New Testament, in
four instances it concerned economic exploitation and abuses
of power, not same-sex behavior; or more precisely, perhaps,

---

33 Michael Vasey, *Strangers and Friends: A New Exploration of
Homosexuality and the Bible* (London: Hodder & Stoughton, 1995), p.
132.

economic exploitation and violence in the sex business, as in pimping and forced prostitution.[34]

(Check the *Sibylline Oracles, Acts of John,* and *To Autolycus.*)

But then neither would they know that William Loader's magisterial study says it is probably better to take the term as having a broader range than that.[35]

But what then to make of New Testament scholar James Brownson's attention to the fact that the vice list in 1 Timothy 1:10 "includes three interrelated terms in reference to male-male erotic activity"? He puts them together to suggest that the list is collectively referring to "kidnappers or slave dealers (*andropodistai*) acting as 'pimps' for their captured and castrated boys (the *pornoi,* or male prostitutes) servicing the *arsenokoitai,* the men who make use of these boy prostitutes."[36]

Clear yet?

How might the history of Christian treatment of gays and lesbians have been different if *arsenokoitai* had been translated "sex traffickers" or "sexual exploiters" or "rapists" or "sexual predators" or "pimps"? Such translations are plausible, even if not the majority scholarly reconstruction at this time. And they are at least as adequate, or inadequate, as "homosexuals"—a term from *our* culture with a range of meanings including sexual orientation, identity and activity—not a word from Paul's world.

It might have been nice if in our English Bibles the genuine uncertainty about how to translate Paul's neologism *arsenokoitai,* or the two words *malakoi* and *arsenokoitai* together, at least had been mentioned in a footnote.

---

34 Dale B. Martin, *Sex and the Single Savior: Gender and Sexuality in Biblical Interpretation* (Louisville: Westminster John Knox, 2006), p. 39.
35 Loader, *New Testament on Sexuality,* pp. 330-331.
36 James V. Brownson, *Bible, Gender, Sexuality: Reframing the Church's Debate on Same-Sex Relationships* (Grand Rapids: William B. Eerdmans Publishing Company, 2013), p. 274.

But alas ... most of the translations we got, read as if every homosexual person was being condemned—to eternal fire. This overly confident translation decision then shadowed the lives of all LGBT people, most sadly gay and lesbian adolescents rejected by their mothers and fathers (and pastors and youth ministers) as hell-bound perverts.

Very high-level scholarly uncertainty about the meaning and translation of these two Greek words, together with profound cultural and linguistic differences, undermines claims to the conclusiveness of *malakoi* and *arsenokoitai* for resolving the LGBT issue.

I deeply lament the damage done by certain questionable and sometimes crudely derogatory Bible translations in the lives of vulnerable people made in God's image.

CHAPTER 14

God Made Them Male and Female

We turn to the most important texts for the LGBT issue—Genesis 1-2, Matthew 19, Romans 1—and the most significant theological issue: God's design for sexuality in creation.

THERE ARE ONLY four passages of Scripture widely quoted on the traditionalist side that I have not yet considered: Genesis 1:26-28/2:18-25, Matthew 19:3-12 (and parallels), and Romans 1:26-27.

Despite differences in content and background, they are all (mainly) relevant to the LGBT debate in the same way: *all have been read to suggest the illegitimacy of same-sex relationships based on God's original design for human sexuality in creation, often defined as male/female sexual/gender complementarity.*[37]

---

37 This is the leading argument of the primary contemporary traditionalist scholar, Robert A.J. Gagnon. See his *The Bible and Homosexual Practice: Texts and Hermeneutics* (Nashville: Abingdon Press, 2001). Similarly, see William J. Webb, *Slaves, Women & Homosexuals: Exploring the Hermeneutics of Cultural Analysis* (Downers Grove, IL: Intervarsity Press, 2001), ch. 5.

This design renders all same-sex relations as "out of order," that is, contrary to God's fixed plan for creation.[38]

This is clearly the single most important biblical-theological-ethical issue faced by any Christian wrestling with the LGBT issue. It is very widely cited on the traditionalist side. It deserves careful consideration.

Finalized probably during and after the Jewish exile in Babylon (587-539 B.C.), the function of Genesis as a whole was mainly to clarify and reinforce a distinctive and unifying Jewish origins story, theological narrative and ethical vision, drawing both on their own historic traditions and to some extent on the traditions of their neighbors. In Genesis 1-11, a primeval prehistory, the authors/editors both borrowed from and subverted their neighbors' creation stories, while adding new elements, to paint a theological picture of creation and human origins, marriage and family life, the sources of human evil and suffering, the birth of culture, agriculture, early technology, and cities, the origins of diverse peoples and languages and the conditions existing on planet Earth prior to the call of Abraham—all framed as a story of a good creation made by God, damaged by human rebellion, subjected to God's judgment, and yet also offered divine redemption.

Most scholars agree that Genesis 1:1-2:4a and 2:4b-25 are two different creation accounts interwoven by an editor. Genesis 1:26-28 says humans are made in the image of God, created with "sexual difference"[39] as male and female, and commanded (blessed) to be fruitful, multiply, fill the earth, and "subdue" it. Genesis 2:18-25 depicts God's recognition of the loneliness of

38 Donald J. Wold, *Out of Order: Homosexuality in the Bible and the Ancient Near East* (Grand Rapids: Baker, 1998).
39 See Catholic theological ethicist Christopher Chennault Roberts, *Creation and Covenant: The Significance of Sexual Difference in the Moral Theology of Marriage* (New York/London, T & T Clark, 2007). He concludes that sexual difference matters a great deal, which contributes to his rejection of revisionism on the LGBT issue.

the original man and his need for a helper/companion/part-ner; taken from the man's rib, this partner is woman. The final two verses function etiologically to explain the origins of mar-riage, as the first man and woman are called "man" and "wife."

So there they are, two ancient, truly lovely accounts of God's creation of humanity and of the first couple. An extraor-dinarily elaborate literature in biblical studies, theology and ethics has been written based on these brief ancient accounts, related to God's purposes in creation, what it means to be made in the image of God, what human responsibility for cre-ation looks like, how the procreation mandate/blessing is to be understood in a world now filled with seven billion people, how intrinsically relational human beings are ("not good to be alone"), the nature of humanity's relationship with the other creatures made by God, and the kind of relationship God intended between that original man and woman.

The fact that it is a man and a woman, and only a man and a woman, referenced in the discussions of sex and marriage in Genesis 1-2—and the fact that only a man and a woman have been able to procreate (until reproductive technology came along)—has been pivotal in shaping traditional Chris-tian opinion on the LGBT issue. Christian tradition has taken these texts as prescriptive for all times and all peoples pertain-ing to the design and purpose of sex, marriage and family life. That has excluded those who are unable to fulfill that prescrip-tion due to their sexual orientation. But increasingly today it is noted that core practices referred to in Genesis 1-2, includ-ing mutual care for children, helper-partner companionship (Genesis 2:18) and total self-giving, can and do occur among covenanted gay and lesbian couples.

～

Jesus' teaching on divorce as recorded in Matthew 5:31-32, 19:3-12//Mark 10:2-12 (and Luke 16:18) is simple in its way, but appears to have become more complex in the Gospel writers' editing process. I have written about these texts at length elsewhere.[40]

Suffice it to say the following here: When Jesus is asked whether it is "lawful for a man to divorce his wife" (for any cause—Matthew 19:3), he leads the conversation back to Old Testament sources. "Moses" (Deuteronomy 24:1-4) is cited but trumped by a composite Jesus offers of Genesis 1:27 and 2:24. Jesus adds his famous ruling, "Therefore what God has joined together, let no one separate" (Matthew 10:6b//Mark 10:9). Jesus then goes on to condemn (illegitimate?) divorce-initiation and remarriage as adultery.

In Matthew's version, this then triggers a conversation with the disciples where they seem taken aback by the strictness of this teaching, such that it might be "better not to marry" (Matthew 19:10). Jesus responds by suggesting the new possibility in a Jewish context of becoming "eunuchs for the kingdom," which seems to mean embracing celibacy. This passage matters quite a bit for *authorizing* a celibacy option in Christianity. Some Christians, including some gay Christians, read it as *mandating* celibacy for all gays and lesbians. Such claims carry more existential weight when they come from celibate gay Christians—as they sometimes do—than from straight Christians enjoying the pleasures of married life.

The goal of this teaching-then-text was not to address what we now call the LGBT issue, though it is sometimes cited in that debate because Jesus references Genesis 1-2. The text itself intends a stern attack on the growing tendency toward permissiveness in first-century Jewish practice, allowing men to initiate divorce from their wives for trivial reasons, leaving families shattered and women disgraced and destitute. So the purpose of his teaching was to call listeners to a much stricter understanding of the permanence of marriage, which God intended to be a lifelong one-flesh relationship for the good

---

40 See Glen H. Stassen and David P. Gushee, *Kingdom Ethics* (Downers Grove, IL: Intervarsity Press, 2003), ch. 13, and David P. Gushee, *Getting Marriage Right* (Grand Rapids: Baker, 2004).

of adults, children and community. That teaching definitely needs to be heard in our churches today. The text's relevance to the LGBT issue is more debated.

~

Scholars historically have agreed that Paul's purpose in Romans 1-3 is to paint a theological picture of the world, leading to the conclusion that every human being desperately needs the salvation offered by God through Jesus Christ. After celebrating the Gospel that saves both Jew and Greek, in Romans 1:18-32 Paul points his accusation primarily toward the characteristic sins of the pagan Gentile population—at its worst, or as he sees it, or for the purposes of this particular theological indictment.

Paul indicts those who quite inexcusably "suppress the truth" about God available in creation (Romans 1:20), dishonoring God by engaging in the futile practices of idol worship. In response, the aggrieved God's punishment is that he "gave them up" to the dishonorable/shameful lusts, impurity and degrading passions that they now desire (Romans 1:24-26). Their consequent spiral downward into moral debasement is then illustrated by yet another vice list, indeed 22 types of vices (Romans 1:26-32) including (vv. 29-31) "every kind of wickedness, evil, covetousness, malice … envy, murder, strife, deceit, craftiness, they are gossips, slanderers, God-haters, insolent, haughty, boastful, inventors of evil, rebellious toward parents, foolish, faithless, heartless, ruthless."

But, fatefully, the one issue Paul singles out for more extended treatment in this passage is same-sex intercourse. Romans 1:26-27 is the most widely cited passage in the entire LGBT debate:

For this reason God gave them up to degrading passions. Their women exchanged natural intercourse for unnatural, and in the same way also the men, giving up natural intercourse with women, were consumed with passion for one another. Men committed shameless acts with men and received in their own persons the due penalty for their error.

Our starting point is of course the constant citation of this verse to describe contemporary gay and lesbian people as having grossly misdirected sexual passions, and to depict all same-sex acts as in the neighborhood of "unnatural," "shameless" and punishable by God. It is a fearsome legacy, especially if one cares about the suffering of those raised in Christian homes and churches who discover a same-sex orientation.

The massive scholarly literature about this text flows in a number of directions, including what background textual or cultural influences shaped Paul's claims here, what specific terms like "natural and unnatural" mean for him, what Paul was intending to teach in his context (exegesis), and what we are to make of it in our own time (hermeneutics and ethics).

Backgrounds: The always fair-minded William Loader suggests that Paul's Jewish background is probably primary, including the Leviticus texts we considered earlier as well as the creation narratives. Paul may also be attempting to integrate Greco-Roman intellectual and moral thinking, as in Stoicism, related to the "natural" and universal access to knowledge of the natural. And any review of what is known of Roman sexual practices and norms, including the wide acceptance of same-sex acts in various circumstances, including by married men, demonstrates their dramatic variance from traditional Jewish sexual ethics.[41]

Loader further suggests cultural themes, which might have affected Paul and would be less familiar or welcome to

---

41 William Loader, *The New Testament on Sexuality* (Grand Rapids: William B. Eerdmans Publishing Company, 2012), p. 315.

contemporary Christian traditionalist readers. One of these is an honor/shame concern related to men giving up their superior, active role in sex and allowing themselves to be treated like women. Another is the common association of male-male sex with humiliating, violent rape, often in war. As for women, their presumed designed/natural passivity as the recipient of male desire in sex would be shockingly overridden in volitional same-sex acts. It would be a disturbing expression of women's agency in a patriarchal society, and thus viewed as unnatural, and certainly as a threat to male power.[42]

Here are four approaches I have seen that raise questions about the traditional interpretation of what Paul says here:

1. By using the language of "exchanging" or giving up "natural" for "unnatural" intercourse, Paul may be saying that he thinks those engaging in same-sex intercourse were capable of "normal," natural heterosexual relations but perversely chose same-sex. Empirically speaking, this was sometimes true then, as it is now (see next paragraph). But, at the hermeneutical level, we now know that a small sexual minority is not at all capable of heterosexual attraction or relations. It does not seem that they can be fairly described as exchanging or giving up natural for unnatural sex. This raises reasonable questions about the fairness of applying this description to that part of the human community today.

2. We know that same-sex behavior in the Greco-Roman world very often, though not always (scholars differ on how to describe the balance between consensual and coercive/harmful shares of same-sex activity), looked like pederasty, prostitution and master-slave sex. These acts were criticized by pagan moralists and not just Christians. These were primarily indulgences of privileged men who had the power to take and use other people's bodies for pleasure, and the luxury to spend a fair amount of time messing around with all different kinds of sex. For these men, a wife alone was not enough. They wanted novelty, excess, pleasures of ever more exotic

---

42 Loader, *New Testament on Sexuality*, pp. 316-317.

kinds. The first-century Roman philosopher Musonius Rufus, for example, wrote: "Not the least significant part of the life of luxury and self-indulgence lies also in sexual excess ... those who lead such a life crave a variety of loves ... not women alone but also men."[43]

Some argue that Paul is reacting to this culture of sexual excess, selfishness and sanctioned adultery in Romans 1, and that the same-sex part of the problem was incidental rather than central. This claim too is strongly disputed. Its resolution has an impact on a scholar's sense of the relevance of this text to consensual (not to mention loving and covenantal) same-sex relationships.[44]

3. Harvard classics scholar Sarah Ruden, in her bracing book *Paul Among the People*, sharpens the cultural issue considerably.[45] Quoting all kinds of sources, including popular as well as high poetry, she describes widespread and quite vile Greco-Roman cultural practices authorizing often violent anal rape of powerless young men, especially slaves, but really anybody of lower social status. This practice was cruelly accompanied by *moral condemnation of the victims rather than the victimizers*, the latter of which were often celebrated for their virility. She documents how young boys had to be very carefully protected from sexual attacks, which could happen at any time, humiliating them emotionally and perhaps destroying them physically. Ruden is convinced that this is what Paul had in mind when he thought about same-sex interest and activity, and this is why he links it to other vices of excess and debauchery in Romans 1. She claims Paul's teachings on sexuality are in large part reflective of revulsion at this kind of cultural depravity, his desire to protect the

43 Musonius Rufus, "On Sexual Matters," quoted in Matthew Vines, *God and the Gay Christian* (New York: Convergent, 2014), p. 38.
44 As claims James V. Brownson, *Bible, Gender, Sexuality: Reframing the Church's Debate on Same-Sex Relationships* (Grand Rapids: William B. Eerdmans Publishing Company, 2013), p. 261.
45 Sarah Ruden, *Paul Among the People: The Apostle Reinterpreted and Reimagined in His Own Time* (New York: Image Books, 2010), ch. 3.

bodies and souls of the innocent, and his commitment to disciplining young Christians who would not participate in this vicious and widespread behavior. If this was his goal, no one could have a dispute with Paul. We could all agree that a culture like this is depraved.

4. Paul was writing to Roman Christians, some of whom had connections in the Roman imperial court, and all of whom would be familiar with the craziness there. The violence, carousing and orgiastic sexuality of that court, including Gaius Caligula's many depravities and Nero's own same-sex relations, were legendary.[46]

James Brownson describes this cruel licentiousness in detail, noting that it may also explain the (oft-abused) line here in Romans 1:27 about "men...receiv[ing] in their own persons the due penalty for their error." Caligula, who raped the wives of dinner guests, had same-sex encounters and sexually humiliated a military officer, was in turn stabbed through the genitals when he was assassinated.[47]

If Paul had the imperial court in mind while painting his broad brushstrokes about the idolatrous debauchery of the Gentile world, that would mean that Romans 1:18-32 (look at that whole description again in this light) might have functioned as a highly evocative, deeply contextual, thinly veiled depiction of the Roman imperial court as a macabre worst-case symbol of Gentile depravity. This connects to a broader theme in recent Pauline scholarship about Paul's defiance of the Roman Empire in the name of the one Lord, Jesus Christ. This really important discovery would limit the applicability of this text for contemporary circumstances that are far different than the Roman court.

A gently revisionist conclusion would be to suggest that Paul's theological purpose in Romans 1, and the religious and cultural context that he swam in when he wrote it, precluded him from speaking sympathetically about any kind

46 Loader, *New Testament on Sexuality*, p. 300.
47 Brownson, *Bible, Gender, Sexuality*, pp. 156-157.

of same-sex relationships. The "subject" may seem to be the same, but many have argued that the context is so different that Paul's words are of little relevance to the question of covenanted same-sex relations among devoted Christians. This would not be the only subject on which the contemporary application of Paul's statements have been reevaluated in this way, leading to the setting aside of his implied or explicit directives (head-coverings, hair, women keeping silent in church, instructions to slaves to obey their masters).

Such a conclusion is not compelling to traditionalists, who link Paul's teaching here to the other texts in the canon that we have explored, notably the creation/design theme, thus decontextualizing Paul's teaching considerably and viewing it as part of a coherent overall biblical sexual ethic.

Still, stepping back, it is appropriate to wonder whether what Paul is so harshly condemning in Romans 1 has much if anything to do with that devout, loving lesbian couple who have been together 20 years and sit on the third row at church. Their lives do not at all look like the overall picture of depravity offered in Romans 1:18-32. You certainly wonder about this when you know that couple—or when you *are* that couple.

Next we will look much more closely at the theme of God's design in creation and how it relates to sexual orientation.

CHAPTER 15

Creation, Sexual Orientation and God's Will

*Three proposals for thinking about creation,
sexual orientation and God's will.*

HERE ARE THREE potential proposals for responding to the very important claim that *God's design in creation rules out any legitimate same-sex relationships*, a claim derived from Genesis 1-2, Matthew 19, Romans 1, and perhaps also Leviticus 18/20 and 1 Corinthians 6:9/1 Timothy 1:10. Nearly every biblical exploration in this book so far has been leading us to this point. These proposals are offered in recognition that theologically, this is the ultimate fork in the road related to the LGBT issue.

Proposal 1: Treat Old Testament creation accounts, and any New Testament allusions or references to them, as theological accounts rather than scientific descriptions of the world as we find it. This requires faithful contemporary Christians to find ways to integrate two different kinds of knowledge—as we (sometimes) have done before, in relation to other issues.

Essentially, this proposal suggests that the LGBT issue is a faith/science integration issue.

Since the 16th century, Christians, Jews and Muslims have faced a major fork in the road concerning to what extent we are able or willing to integrate the findings of science with our primal creation narratives and the theological traditions that we have developed from them. The problem is similar in kind today to what it was when Scripture, Christian tradition and its authoritative interpreters first confronted Galileo, Copernicus and Darwin.[48]

Just as Christians have had to come to terms with an earth that stubbornly continues to revolve around the sun rather than the other way around (as it was believed that Scripture taught), and with a multi-billion-year evolutionary process rather than a 6,000-year-old Earth and a literal six 24-hour-days creation, on the LGBT issue we face the challenge of integrating contemporary scientific findings about gender and sexual orientation into our theological story of the world God made. It has never been easy for Christians to do this integration of biblical text with stubbornly resistant facts out there in our world. It isn't easy now.

We *know* that Genesis 1 says "God made them male and female" and blessed them with the ability to be fruitful and multiply. This makes sense, and we run into lots of clearly male and clearly female people and their offspring every day. But we also now *know* from real human beings and research about them that a very small percentage of the human population is intersexual or transgender. (Intersex: a variation in sex characteristics involving chromosomes, gonads or genitals that do not allow a person to be distinctly identified as male or female. Transgender: a person whose gender identity or expression does not match their assigned sex.)

---

48 I am grateful to Matthew Vines for triggering this initial insight in relation to Galileo. See his *God and the Gay Christian* (New York: Convergent Books, 2014), pp. 21-25.

These phenomena, embodied by real people, exist. How are we to integrate these stubborn facts with Scripture, while responding compassionately to the real human beings in front of us?

We *know* that Genesis 2 says that God made the woman from the man, gave the woman to the man, and declared that the male and the female together make a marriage. This makes sense, and we run into lots of clearly male and clearly female people needing each other, wanting each other and partnering with each other all the time. But we also *know* from real human beings and research about them that about 3.4 to 5 percent of the population cannot find a "suitable partner" (Genesis 2) in a member of the "opposite sex" because that is not their (fixed, enduring, unchangeable) sexual orientation. (Even if we reduce the number to 2 percent to account for bisexuals and some measure of sexual-orientation fluidity, the point still holds for the 2 percent.) Meanwhile we ought to *know* that a predictably very large percentage of these irresistibly attracted same-sex people have the same aching need for partnership and sexual companionship, and the same aching grief over being alone, that the man experiences, and God recognizes as "not good," in Genesis 2.

These phenomena, embodied by real people, exist. How are we to integrate these stubborn facts with Scripture, while responding compassionately to the real human beings in front of us?

There are only three possible kinds of Christian responses to these two different kinds of knowledge, one offered in the biblical text and the other offered in *stubborn facts* offered by lives and scientific research.

One response seeks to reduce the cognitive dissonance by *throwing out the biblical story as an ancient fable.*

Another seeks to reduce the cognitive dissonance by *throwing out the stubborn facts, such as the reported experiences of real contemporary people, and related research, as godless or impossible.*

The third is to *find some way to integrate both kinds of knowledge,* as many Christians have previously done in relation to a heliocentric solar system and some kind of evolutionary process over billions of years.

A simple way to bring such integration is to say that *normally,* gender identity is clearly male or female and that *normally,* gender identity matches gender assignment and that *normally,* sexual orientation is heterosexual. That is to say, this is statistically what most people experience, and thus the way that most societies have structured their marital, sexual and familial expectations, and thus the account most likely to be reflected in ancient religious texts, including the Bible.

But it is a stubborn fact that difference also exists in the human family, and not just in the area of sexuality. That small minority of people whose gender identity and sexual orientation turn out to be something different than the majority ought to be able to be accepted for who they are, and assisted, where necessary, in the ways most congruent with their overall well-being. This better reflects the spirit of Christ's ministry than demanding an impossible uniformity and rejecting those who do not achieve it.

~

Proposal 2: Because arguments from God's purported design in creation have proven remarkably problematic in Christian history, do not rely on them for sexual ethics.

Essentially, this proposal suggests that Christians should look forward rather than backward when thinking theologically-ethically about the LGBT issue.

I noticed in working through the writings of Dietrich Bonhoeffer in 2013 that after initially accepting the language of "orders of creation" drawn from his Lutheran tradition, he abandoned it for a new language of "mandates."[49]

---

49 See Dietrich Bonhoeffer, *Ethics: Dietrich Bonhoeffer Works, Volume 6* (Minneapolis: Fortress Press Press, 2005, pp. 388-408; see also

He did this at least in part because he had become alarmed by the dangers of orders of creation language in his increasingly Nazified German Christian context. There, many Christians had long defended conservative and even reactionary social conditions as reflecting God's will in creation. Then, in the 1920s and 1930s, Nazi or Nazi-influenced thinkers took concepts such as blood, soil, race and nation and linked them to a theological ethic of creation, adapting Lutheran orders of creation language for this purpose. Thus, it was claimed, and by some top-ranking theologians, that God established different races, of different bloods, in different lands, with a racial hierarchy among the different groups, with a consequent divine prohibition of "race mixing," and so on.

Bonhoeffer instead shifted to mandates language. His approach retained recognition that life comes to us structured in various important institutions or spheres such as family, state and people. But he rejected any claim that what we see around us in a fallen world is simply equal to what God originally created or intended. And he rejected the Nazis' version of what God originally intended. And, finally, he deemphasized creation as an ethical category in favor of the realistic earthly preservation of the conditions of life necessary for human well-being and preparation for Jesus Christ.

This issue reminds me of debates in my own lifetime in which claims from the creation narratives have been used and abused:

- Christians who claim from Genesis 1:26-31 that God gave humans dominion over the earth to do with as we wish, and thus "creation care" talk is a violation of God's plan for human dominion over creation.
- Christians who claim from Genesis 9:11 that God promised never again to send another flood, so the climatologists'

Clifford J. Green, "Editor's Introduction to the English Edition," pp. 17-22.

fear that runaway climate change might change sea levels must be rejected.

• Christians who claim from Genesis 2 that woman is to man as submissive helper to divinely established leader—and from Genesis 3 that woman was "first in the Edenic fall" and therefore morally inferior.

• Christians who claim, or once claimed, that in Genesis 9 the "curse of Ham" means that all those of African descent were destined to be slaves.

I am not suggesting from these sad examples that Genesis 1-11 can play no constructive role in Christian ethics. But I am suggesting the idea that *Christian theology does better leaning forward toward Jesus Christ,* his person and his work, his way of doing ministry and advancing God's coming kingdom, the new creation he brings forth, rather than leaning backward to the primeval creation narratives, where we so often run into trouble.[50]

∾

Proposal 3: Instead of relying just on Genesis 1-2, we should consider more seriously the implications for sexual ethics of living in a Genesis 3 world.

Essentially, this proposal suggests that there can be no actual or theological return to the primeval Garden briefly depicted in the beginning of Genesis.

Historically, most Christians have read Genesis 3 as an account of a primeval human "fall" into sin, and Genesis 4 to Revelation 22 as illustrating the consequences of the fall and God's redemptive response with Israel and in Christ. Let's stay within that thought world for a moment here, even while

---

50 After writing this sentence, I saw a similar claim in James V. Brownson, *Bible, Gender, Sexuality: Reframing the Church's Debate on Same-Sex Relationships* (Grand Rapids: William B. Eerdmans Publishing Company, 2013), p. 269.

recognizing that its exegetical foundation in Genesis 1-3 is arguable.

Many Christian thinkers have said something like this: God creates a good creation, human beings sin and mess it up, and then God acts to offer redemption, a process which will continue until the end of time when Christ returns. We can still see glimpses of the original good creation, we can certainly see plenty of evidence of sin and its disordering effects, and we certainly hope we can see glimpses (or more) of the redemption breaking in through Christ. This remains a theological account I find deeply compelling.

A suitably dark theology of sin recognizes "total depravity," which means that there is no aspect of human or planetary life unaffected by sin and its disordering effects. This would certainly include human sexuality, which is distorted and disordered in a thousand different ways. Think about the sexual offenses and scandals that surface in each week's news. But it is just as true of all aspects of creation and of human life. A sunny liberal optimism about human nature is out of sync with the Christian theological tradition and the evidence of our eyes. It is also out of sync with the strenuous moral exhortations offered throughout Scripture to the people of God, and the obvious limits of those exhortations in bringing fundamental transformation to sinful human beings—even when those human beings are attempting to cooperate.

My suggestion here is simply this: Traditionalists appeal to Genesis 1-2; God made them male and female and male for female, and so everyone needs to conform to this pattern or live as a celibate. But they rarely mention Genesis 3, which (most Christians have said) tells the story of the beginnings of human sin, with the disordering consequences that are so painfully described in Genesis 4 through Revelation.

If we live in a Genesis 3 world, and not a Genesis 1-2 world, this undoubtedly means that *everyone's* sexuality is sinful, broken and disordered, just like everything else about us. Nobody has Genesis 1-2 sexuality. To paraphrase former defense secretary Donald Rumsfeld (surprised you there, didn't I?), *we go into adult life with the sexuality we have, not the sexuality we might want or wish to have.* No adult is a sexual innocent. Our task, if we are Christians, is to attempt to order the sexuality we have in as responsible a manner as we can. We can't get back to Genesis 1-2, a primal sinless world. But we can do the best we can with the Genesis 3 sexuality we have. Catholic ethicist Lisa Cahill once wrote that Christian sexual ethics in the world we actually live in must help people come to "the most morally commendable course of action concretely available" in their particular circumstances.[51]

That pertains to all of us.

Traditionalists often speak as if heterosexual people's sexuality is innocent while gay and lesbian people's sexuality is broken/damaged/sinful. Revisionists often speak as if everyone's sexuality is innocent. *I am suggesting that in Genesis 3 perspective, no one's sexuality is innocent.* Everyone's sexuality is broken in ways known quite well to each of us in our own hearts. Everyone's sexuality needs to be morally disciplined and ordered. Meanwhile, basic standards of Christian humility direct our attention to our own issues rather than those of others.

I will argue in the next chapter that the Christian tradition has already proposed a norm for human beings wrestling with Genesis 3 sexuality: that norm is covenant. It is a rigorous standard, challenging us to the most strenuous effort, and constantly flouted today, including by Christians.

If we really care about getting our sexual ethics right in a Genesis 3 world, we need a sturdy recommitment to covenant. It is a standard that all of us can strive for, and be measured by.

---

51 Lisa Sowle Cahill, *Between the Sexes: Foundations for a Christian Ethics of Sexuality* (Philadelphia: Fortress Press Press/New York: Paulist Press), 1985, p. 148.

CHAPTER 16

Toward Covenant

*What next? Exploring a covenantal standard
for every Christian's sexual ethics.*

MANY CHRISTIAN COLLEGES and seminaries are wrestling with the LGBT issue. Frequently in my visits to these schools over the last two decades this ubiquitous issue has come up, even when it is not on the agenda.

I remember one time I was doing a workshop at a very conservative Christian college out west. Our conversation "went there." I recall this crystalline observation from a philosopher on that faculty: "The problem is that we know that homosexuality is wrong, but we don't know why anymore." And philosophers, of all people, know that if you can't make an argument for your claim, but can only make an assertion, you are in an untenable position.

Parents know this too, in their own way. I remember participating in a parenting seminar grounded in materials written by a quite conservative evangelical. One of the things I liked about that material was the author's emphasis on parents *giving reasons* to their children for the rules they were imposing.

So: Those who are ineradicably gay or lesbian in their sexual orientation must never develop romantic relationships, because … why, exactly? What are the reasons? What might make such relationships sinful? To use James Brownson's phrase, what is the "moral logic" of this prohibition?[52]

The Bible says so. Okay, which passages exactly?

- Genesis 19/Judges 19: But these texts teach how horrible it is to gang rape visiting men/angels. Unfortunately, Sodom became associated with "sodomy" for a thousand years.

- Leviticus 18/20: These texts say men lying with men as with women is an abomination, but scholars differ as to what the reasons for this ban were. My chapter discussed the complexity of developing Christian ethical norms from these and other Old Testament legal texts.

- 1 Corinthians 6/1 Timothy 1: These texts offer two Greek words whose meanings are somewhat unclear and doubtfully translated, and place them in vice lists with few context clues.

- Genesis 1-2/Matthew 19/Romans 1 (maybe also Leviticus 18/20, 1 Corinthians 6/1 Timothy 1): These texts can be read to say that same-sex relationships violate God's design in creation, often described as sexual complementarity, even though such readings are also debatable. Still, this is the strongest "why" on the traditionalist side. In my last chapter, I offered three possible responses to this one strong surviving reason to morally reject all same-sex relationships (and earlier I discussed important cultural background factors contributing to Paul's treatment of same-sex issues).

Traditionalists sometimes express wonderment about how any Christian could reconsider their view on the LGBT issue. But here's one source of the reconsideration: The purported biblical *reasons* for the ban on the only kind of

---

52 James V. Brownson, *Bible, Gender, Sexuality: Reframing the Church's Debate on Same-Sex Relationships* (Grand Rapids: William B. Eerdmans Publishing Company, 2013), p. 259.

helper-partner-romantic relationships that gay and lesbian people could ever pursue mainly come down to a single core theological claim based on creation texts and a handful of possible echoes and allusions in the New Testament.

And on the basis of this reading of Scripture, reinforced through Christian tradition, wired into the power structures of very-difficult-to-change ecclesiastical authorities in global Christianity, creating a deep inertia in Christian ways of thinking and acting, a small 3.4 to 5 percent minority of our brothers and sisters in Christ have been excluded from full acceptance into Christian community. All too often they have been disowned and hounded out of their own families. They have been subjected to severe psychological distress and driven to self-harm and suicide. And in society, gays and lesbians have suffered civil discrimination for centuries, which is only now easing, with some Christians fighting any such easing tooth and nail. That's a big price to pay.

Having reviewed the relevant texts carefully, I now believe that what has been viewed as unassailable biblical evidence for the moral marginalization of LGBT people or those in same-sex relationships is not so indisputable after all. *It mainly depends on whether we can think differently about how to relate our Christian account of God's design in creation with the existence of a small minority of gay and lesbian neighbors, some of whom are devout followers of Christ.* Certainly I believe such a conversation should not be impossible; the matter should not be beyond dialogue and study, some of which I have attempted here.

Move forward with me toward another fork in the road. Let's say we pull LGBT people back from outer darkness and include them in Christian community like everyone else. This does not resolve the question of what LGBT people are actually supposed to do with their sexual and romantic longings. Let's say the ban-based-on-orientation is lifted. What goes in its place? That also requires a proposal, and reasons why.

≈

Much of contemporary western culture would say: An appropriate sexual ethic is to do whatever you want to do sexually if it doesn't hurt anybody who doesn't want to get hurt while having sex—or perhaps, with a bit more refinement, if it doesn't involve the exploitation of a minor or an impaired person or doesn't risk pregnancy or disease. Let's call this the *mutual consent ethic*. Other than that, anything goes.

Some, refining their ethic to a somewhat higher and more demanding level, would say: An appropriate sexual ethic is to find a person to love, and to restrict sex only to that person for as long as that relationship shall last. Let's call this the *loving relationship ethic.*

Christianity has historically said: God's plan for sexual ethics requires a man and a woman to make a binding lifetime marriage covenant with each other (before God, church and state, representing civil society), and to remain faithful to the promises of that covenant, including fidelity and exclusivity, until one partner dies a natural death. Let's call this the *covenantal-marital ethic.* It bans all non-marital sex, infidelity, abandonment and divorce (with rare exceptions), making celibacy the only alternative to marriage.

Each sexual ethic corresponds to some need in human life, but each successively requires more of the "Genesis 3" human beings to whom it is applied.

The mutual consent ethic recognizes profound human desires and needs for sex and only sets restrictions related to coercion, abuse and harm. It has a wide impact on our contemporary culture. This is the ethic being taught (apparently quite unsuccessfully, judging by sexual assault rates) on our secular college campuses.

The loving relationship ethic recognizes the same profound human needs for sex, but adds a human capacity for love, and recognizes the human connections and therefore vulnerabilities created between people in an intimate sexual relationship. It recognizes that relationships do better if they are monogamous as long as they last, but it does not expect them to last. This is the ethic taught in most of our love songs.

The Christian covenantal-marital ethic recognizes those desires for sex, and that capacity for love, and that need for fidelity—and also the profound joy possible in a lifetime relationship. But it *demands* that such relationships take the form of marriage, and that those marriages actually last for a lifetime (with certain rare exceptions), even though that is very, very hard for fickle, combative human beings to accomplish. Thus, the Christian tradition did not leave human beings to our own damaged natural inclinations, but surrounded us with legal, moral, communal and ecclesial structures to make us hold fast to our commitments even when we did not want to do so. And it promised the aid of the Christian church and the God we worship for those who sought to make and keep marital covenants.[53]

The covenantal-marital ethic formerly taught by Christian tradition gradually collapsed in the mid-to-late 20th century. You can see it in the generations. My father just buried my mother. They were married for 53 years. They did it right. But few of the generation currently under the age of 35 will ever see a 50-year marriage again. My take is that the mutual consent ethic challenged the covenantal-marital ethic in the 1960s, and the effort of many to compromise with a loving relationship ethic failed badly, producing only serial monogamy at best. But marriage is not really marriage when it is serial monogamy, and the collapse of the very concept of binding, faithful, lifetime covenant has weakened marriage at its foundations. This collapse of the concept of lifetime covenant marriage is without question the greatest sexual-familial ethical issue of our time, and it is the issue that should attract

53 I am intentionally rejecting here any weakening of a covenantal-marital sexual ethics norm. Much contemporary Christian sexual ethics seems to me to represent at least a subtle weakening of that norm. For a leading example, see Margaret Farley, *Just Love: A Framework for Christian Sexual Ethics* (New York/London: Continuum, 2006).

the moral scrutiny that has instead come to be focused on the LGBT issue.

In a culture with collapsing (or never-formed) marriages, it is children who suffer the most. The forgotten element in contemporary Christian thinking about marriage is children. It is as if the adults of the 1960s just forgot the procreative power of sex. Adults could have sex with whomever they wanted whenever they wanted because the pill or the condom would take care of it.

But it didn't. Half of the children in the U.S. are conceived accidentally, and about 40 percent are born out of wedlock. And divorce is pretty much ubiquitous. And so all over America, and all over the "advanced" world, powerless children are tossed like flotsam and jetsam in and out of the chaotic sexual lives of their parents. The cunning genius of the older covenantal-marital ethic was that it was at least as much about the well-being of children as adults.

I am a covenantal-marital sexual ethics guy. Anybody who has ever read anything I have previously written on this subject will know that. I think this ethic emerges from Scripture in texts like Malachi 2, Matthew 19/Mark 10, and Ephesians 5. I loathe the mutual consent ethic; I think it is disastrous. I am sure the loving relationship ethic ultimately fails as well. I think that the best reading of the witness of Scripture, as well as the evidence available to our own eyes, is that human beings—adults and children—need marital covenants that last a lifetime. I am at the 30-year mark of my own Christian marriage covenant. And I am the very blessed recipient of the great covenant made by my parents.

The explorations of these many chapters have not shaken that commitment in the slightest. I am a strict covenantalist and have little patience with Christian churches that lack the confidence and rigor to take a demanding covenantal approach. I also think that their moral looseness has badly hurt the serious Christian LGBT community that wants in on classic Christianity (minus the anti-gay stuff).

There are some liberal gay, lesbian and bisexual Christians who want me and other Christian pastor-scholar types to offer unequivocal "welcome and affirmation" to whatever sexual relationships they feel like embarking upon. They will not find it from me.

But, there are also gay, lesbian, and yes, bisexual Christians who are asking to be grafted into the covenantal-marital ethic of the Christian tradition. They want to make a lifetime covenant with one person, in keeping with the witness of the Christian tradition, and they would like some support from their congregations in doing so.

Bisexual— Like dogs

It is actually rather remarkable—despite their rejection at the hands of the Church, these quite "traditionalist" gays and lesbians have embraced the Church's own very best teaching about marriage and covenant. They just want a place in that tradition too.

In exploring the LGBT issue here, I have never asked whether the disciplined covenantal-marital standard in Christian sexual ethics should be weakened to "affirm" whatever casual, exploitative, experimental, out-of-control, drunk, hookup, polyamorous, sex-while-dating, or follow-your-heart sexual practices are bouncing around American culture, mainly among heterosexuals.

I am instead asking whether devout gay and lesbian Christians might be able to participate in the covenantal-marital sexual ethical standard—one person, for life, faithful and exclusive, in a loving, nonexploitative, noncoercive, reciprocal relationship, that is the highest expression of Christian sexual ethics—which, in fact, a goodly number are already doing. I can't find a compelling reason to say no anymore.

CHAPTER 17

Transformative Encounters and Paradigm Leaps

How paradigm shifts (or leaps) in biblical interpretation have often occurred through surprising encounters with God and people.

IN THE LAST few chapters I have gradually sought to reveal why traditionalist ways of connecting the biblical dots on the LGBT issue no longer are compelling to me.

It could seem as if I am arguing that my whole process of rethinking this issue has been nothing other than a matter of biblical study. I once studied the Bible and it read this way to me; now I study the Bible and it reads a new way to me.

But my own ethical methodology has never been that naïve. In *Kingdom Ethics*, we offer a four-box diagram originally developed by Glen Stassen related to how moral discernment occurs.[54]

We say that basic convictions, loyalties, trusts, interests, passions, ways of perceiving reality and ways of moral

54 Glen H. Stassen and David P. Gushee, *Kingdom Ethics: Following Jesus in Contemporary Context* (Downers Grove, IL: Intervarsity Press, 2003), p. 59.

reasoning are complexly interconnected, and that this involves head and heart, not just rational cogitation. The final few chapters will mainly be working at this level.

I was doing my devotional reading while on vacation last summer—I made sure to say both of those things so readers wondering about my salvation are at least aware that I still read the Bible devotionally, even on vacation—and I was utterly dumbstruck by something I had never noticed before about the Emmaus Road story of Luke 24.

In the story, the two heartbroken disciples are discussing with a stranger the shattering of their dreams. Jesus had just been judicially murdered, but they "had hoped that he was the one to redeem Israel" (Luke 24:21). It turns out that the person they are talking with is Jesus himself, but they "were kept from recognizing him" (Luke 24:16). They tell the story as they now see it, and then the mysterious stranger says, "Oh, how foolish you are, and how slow of heart to believe all that the prophets have declared! Was it not necessary that the Messiah should suffer these things and then enter into his glory?" The text goes on to say, "Then beginning with Moses and all the prophets, he interpreted to them the things about himself in all the Scriptures" (Luke 24:26-27). Finally, after a mysteriously sacramental meal with the stranger, "they recognized him" (Luke 24:31), and he vanished.

No biblical scholar argues that first-century Jews expected a crucified Messiah, an undelivered Israel and an untransformed world. Nothing in the birth narratives of Luke (Luke 1-2) shows anyone anticipating that the baby to be born to deliver Israel would do his deliverance by dying naked and derided on a Roman cross. In Jewish-Christian dialogue, the point was made very clearly by my dissertation advisor Rabbi Irving Greenberg when he said Jesus could not have been Messiah for "the overwhelming majority of Jews ... given the facts on the ground."[55]

55 Irving Greenberg, *For the Sake of Heaven and Earth: The New Encounter between Judaism and Christianity* (Philadelphia: Jewish Publication Society, 2004), p. 65.

But for the early Jewish and then Gentile Christians, their transformative encounter with Jesus led them to a huge paradigm shift, so huge it is better to call it a *paradigm leap*. Despite the prior and still-prevailing Jewish interpretation, they now believed that this Jesus actually was the promised Deliverer, Messiah and much more. The way they knew this was because their old paradigm did not survive their transformative encounter with Jesus Christ. Old paradigm + *transformative encounter* = paradigm leap to a new reading of Scripture.

Jewish Christians were those who initially made that paradigm leap after their transformative encounter with Jesus, notably the post-resurrection Jesus. Non-Christian Jews were those who did not, perhaps because they had no such opportunity. It was the birth of a fateful schism, a huge fork in the road if ever there was one.

Consider another really important biblical text.

Many who have been wrestling with this LGBT issue, especially in increasingly "sexual-orientation-integrated" congregations, have found themselves returning to Acts 10. I won't retell the whole story, just the punch line. God teaches Peter through his divinely arranged encounter with the converted Gentile centurion Cornelius that: "God shows no partiality but in every nation anyone who fears him and does what is right is acceptable to him. ... Jesus Christ—he is Lord of all" (Acts 10:34-36).

Peter had operated from a biblical paradigm rooted firmly in widely attested Jewish Scriptures and tradition that God favors the Jewish people through election and that "it is unlawful for a Jew to associate with or visit a Gentile." But: "God has shown me that I should not call anyone profane or unclean" (Acts 10:28). This Biblical paradigm, *plus the divinely arranged transformative encounter with newly converted Gentile believers,* forges a huge paradigm leap, leading to a new reading of Scripture. Any student of the New Testament knows how very difficult this paradigm leap turned out to be for the early Church, including for Peter himself. The Church would now welcome Gentiles on equal terms with Jews, and Jewish law would be largely set aside?! Some were able to make this change; others were not. Another fork in the road.

On that same vacation, I started reading Harriet Beecher Stowe's classic *Uncle Tom's Cabin*. I was floored by how much of that classic abolitionist work is about white Christian arguments related to what Scripture says about slavery. Countless scenes reveal the heartless use of slavery-affirming biblical texts by slave-owners, traders and many others to stiffen the slaveholding spine and also to suppress slave resistance. But in numerous places those quoting these quite clear sentences of Scripture like, "Slaves obey your masters as is fitting in the Lord" (Colossians 3), are *challenged by transformative encounters with actual slaves*—their humanity, their suffering, their dignity, their love for their families—which end up shattering their old ways of reading Scripture.

The same thing has happened time and again in the best moments of Christian history. An older or inadequate way of connecting the biblical dots gets shredded by transformative encounters with real human beings.[56]

In precisely these encounters, many attest to the experience of God's transformative Spirit.[57]

It happened when Spaniards and Portuguese were quoting Scripture to justify the conquest and enslavement of the indigenous peoples of Latin America—though some among them, such as Bartolomé de las Casas, could not accept these

---

56 Jack Rogers pointed out our sad Christian history of "misusing the Bible to justify oppression" long ago in his *Jesus, the Bible, and Homosexuality: Explode the Myths, Heal the Church* (Louisville: Westminster John Knox, 2006).

57 The current work on this subject that strikes this theme most profoundly is Ken Wilson, *A Letter to my Congregation: An evangelical pastor's path to embracing people who are gay, lesbian, and transgender into the company of Jesus* (Canton, MI: Read the Spirit Books, 2014).

readings after transformative encounters with the affected, suffering human beings.[58]

It happened—at last, mainly after the Holocaust—when large swaths of the Christian church at last stopped quoting biblical texts to justify contempt for Jews. A millennia-old "teaching of contempt" essentially disappeared in a single generation. Check out Rosemary Ruether's *Faith and Fratricide* for one essential retelling of that terrible story.[59]

And it happened when centuries-old teachings about women's spiritual and moral inferiority essentially collapsed in the face of Christian feminism, and transformative encounters with women's spiritual gifts, that made the older paradigm implausible. Even traditionalists on that issue edged away from most aspects of that tradition other than (some, contested) limit on women's ministerial leadership offices, functions or roles.[60]

Some of us believe that in our time an older, destructive paradigm based on a particular way of connecting the biblical dots *has not survived the transformative encounters we are having with LGBT fellow Christians*, encounters in which we experience regular and astonishing reminders of God's presence.

If such transformative encounters are so important in looking at issues in a new way, it must make moral conflict

---

58 I tell this story in David P. Gushee. *The Sacredness of Life: Why an Ancient Biblical Vision is Key to the World's Future* (Grand Rapids: William B. Eerdmans Publishing Company, 2013), ch. 6.

59 Rosemary Ruether, *Faith and Fratricide: The Theological Roots of Anti-Semitism* (Minneapolis: Winston Press, 1974).

60 Modern "biblical complementarians" abandoned most of the crudest elements of historic Christian patriarchalism, retreating to the fallback position that men should lead women in church life, without agreeing to the exact limits this places on women. See John Piper and Wayne Grudem, *Recovering Biblical Manhood and Womanhood: A Response to Evangelical Feminism* (Wheaton, IL: Crossway Books, 2012).

inevitable—because, inevitably, not everyone is blessed with such transformative encounters. I have been.

Those of us who are in the process of making a paradigm leap toward full acceptance of LGBT people are sometimes accused of "abandoning the Gospel." This is a very serious charge. Are those who level it saying that the Good News that "in Christ God was reconciling the world to himself" (2 Corinthians 5:19), and that "God so loved the world that he gave his only Son, so that everyone who believes him may not perish but have eternal life" (John 3:16) is compromised when Christians propose a rethinking of one aspect of Christian sexual ethics? That's quite a claim!

Transformative encounters with God, and with the humanity and suffering and dignity of those made in God's image, especially those previously marginalized or rejected, more especially those so mistreated by God's own people, often lead to paradigm leaps—but sadly, never for everybody. *Paradigm leaps divide*, at least in their first stages, and those who make them are often accused of abandoning sacred Scripture. But I strongly reject such a claim, or any accusation of having abandoned the Gospel.

The absurdly wonderful Good News that a crucified Jewish carpenter is the Messiah of Israel and Savior of the entire world, and has come to rescue us, was the first such paradigm leap in the history of Christianity. I believe we Christians actually call it "the Gospel." It transformed the world.

CHAPTER 18

A Dual-Narrative Tour

What is going on here? Two very different ways Christians today are "seeing" shifting attitudes on the LGBT issue.

IN THE SUMMER of 2011, I had the privilege of participating in a visit to Israel and the Palestinian territories under the aegis of Fuller Theological Seminary.

The trip was organized as a "dual-narrative tour." Our guides were young local women, one Israeli Arab and one Israeli Jew. Through their own personal stories, as well as their own way of telling the history and reality of circumstances on the ground, these wonderful young guides taught us that there are (at least) two narratives to describe everything that has gone on and is going on in the land between the Jordan and the Mediterranean.

That trip has come to mind often in recent years as I have pondered the LGBT issue. I propose that responses to this issue fall along dual- (dueling-) narrative lines. These narrative frameworks are so self-evident to most of their adherents that they often find the alternative narrative completely inconceivable—just like Israel/Palestine. They offer two alternate ways of "seeing" what is going on in the contemporary LGBT debate.

Decades ago, theologian H.R. Niebuhr wrote that the first question of ethics is not "What should I do?" but "What is going on here?"[61]

He was on to something. So, *what is in fact going on here?*

Let's call the first answer a *narrative of cultural, ecclesial and moral decline.* I know it well, because I have at times written in this vein and have certainly written about it, including in a book to come out in Fall 2015.[62]

Library of Theological Ethics It can be framed from 30,000 feet as a story of western secularization and the collapse of Christendom, or at least Christian cultural dominance. It can be framed at 15,000 feet as a story of Christian capitulation to theological and ethical liberalism, with the consequent erosion of the vitality of the churches. It can be framed at 5,000 feet as a story of the collapse of historic western/Christian sexual ethics under the assaults of the sexual revolution. All add up to the conviction that following Christ faithfully today demands resistance to this decline.

This narrative sees modern western and U.S. history as mainly a sad story of apostasy from an original Christian core. Rarely focusing on historic conflicts and failures in Christian, western or U.S. history, this story instead focuses on, dreams of or ruminates about a time when Christianity held the dominant position in western and American culture, when Christian theology and morality more often prevailed, and when sexual ethics was understood along traditionalist Christian lines—heterosexual, marital, faithful, permanent, etc. The role of the faithful Christian church is to stand against cultural decline, or at least against the encroachment of such decline into the Church itself.

---

61 H. Richard Niebuhr, *The Responsible Self* (New York: Harper & Row, 1963), p. 60.
62 *Evangelical Social Ethics: Converting America and Its Christians, 1944-2014* (Library of Theological Ethics). With Isaac B. Sharp. Louisville: Westminster John Knox Press, 2015.

From the perspective of this narrative, the LGBT issue is framed as yet one more, and perhaps the most egregious, example of this cultural, ecclesial and moral decline. I myself once wrote (in *Getting Marriage Right*) that the gay rights revolution was one of seven revolutions weakening the historic Christian understanding of marriage. I framed it as connected to the sexual revolution, the dramatic rise in divorce, and so on; to stand up for a strengthening of marriage in the Church at least implicitly required standing against the acceptance even of covenanted gay relationships.[63]

Because I once believed this, I find it very hard to demonize those who still do. And I still believe everything I said there except the part about gay people seeking covenanted relationships.

But there is an alternative answer. Let's call it a *narrative of marginalization, resistance and equality.* At 30,000 feet, this is a story of the sad but constant human tendency to pick out "The Other" for contempt, rejection and mistreatment. At 15,000 feet, this is a story about the ways Christians have so often participated in the damaging mistreatment of those viewed as sinful, marginal or less than—whether women, Jews, native Americans, slaves, African-Americans, Muslims, immigrants, prisoners or others. At 5,000 feet, this is a story about how LGBT people and their allies have gained success in resisting further marginalization and have placed pressure on Church and society to change their attitudes and practices. From within this narrative, the role of the faithful Christian church is compassionate participation in the struggles of LGBT people for inclusion, acceptance and equality.

Which narrative do you find most compelling to explain what is going on here? Which vision of the Church's task in our age? Whichever one it is, do you see how particular exegetical decisions related to particular biblical passages do not fully account for it? *Instead, what we are talking about is how*

---

63 David P. Gushee, *Getting Marriage Right: Realistic Counsel for Saving and Strengthening Marriages* (Grand Rapids: Baker, 2004), ch. 1.

narratives make sense for people of broader patterns of reality as they perceive it.

In general, traditionalist Christians all over the western world are attracted to a narrative of cultural decline, and link the contemporary LGBT issue to that narrative. Especially after so many recognizable defeats on the cultural battlefield, and so much doctrinal and moral confusion in the churches, it is easy to understand why drawing a bright red line on this particular issue strikes some traditionalists as absolutely essential. This is Custer's last stand against the rejection of Christendom, against the loss of Christian dominance in culture, against theological liberalism, and against visibly deteriorating sexual ethics in Church and society, as evidenced by the ubiquity of divorce, cohabitation and the hook-up culture. Many will fight on this front to the last man.

Different kinds of traditionalists located in different ecclesial and cultural settings pick out different aspects of the cultural decline narrative on which to focus. Some are fighting hard against civil gay marriage, others are relentlessly focused on detecting and punishing what they see as doctrinal slippage, and others are more tightly focused on exegetical fights or ecclesial politics. Increasing numbers are turning to the protection of the civil rights of traditionalist Christians themselves, as they watch themselves losing the broader cultural battle.

These are not just "fundamentalists." I find thoughtful scholars and leaders in mainline denominations, or in the U.K. setting, for example, who are reading reality in this particular way. Aware of really quite disturbing cultural trends toward total libertinism, in unhappy community with fellow Christians whose understanding of Christian theology is, one might say, pretty loose, they are worried that even qualified acceptance of devout gay Christians, or covenanted, exclusive, gay relationships, will just be a slippery slope toward (further) cultural, ecclesial and moral decline. So they draw the line right here, and sometimes quite vigorously.

[handwritten margin note:] When you choose between the lesser of two evils Are still you choosing evil.

I understand them. And in many ways I agree with their worries over post-Christian culture, theologically and ethically sloppy Christianity and ever-edgier sexual license. I cringe when I hear people make pro-gay arguments that are little more than individualism and preference-utilitarianism with a bit of religious language slopped on. That's also why I never just use "welcoming and affirming" language about this issue—I need to know what exactly is being affirmed. And it explains why I do not think it is at all a good idea to encourage sexual experimentation and transgressiveness as a positive good, as often seems the spirit on our college campuses and among *avant garde* academicians. Where possible, I think it is best for young people to figure out a clear gender identity and sexual identity and stick with it. (Call me a conservative.)

But my dozens of encounters with serious gay Christians, many of them evangelical, many of them in covenanted relationships, have detached me from the broader declinist narrative as it pertains at least to devoutly Christian LGBT persons. Perhaps my readiness to take these Christian sisters and brothers seriously has also been affected by serious study of numerous instances in the past and today when Christians have read Scripture so as to hurt and marginalize disfavored groups.

If what we are talking about is blessing an anything-goes ethic in a morally libertine culture, I stand utterly opposed, as I have throughout my career. But if what we are talking about is carving out space for serious committed Christians who happen to be gay or lesbian, to participate in society as equals, in church as kin, and in the blessings and demands of covenant on the same terms as everyone else, I now think that has nothing to do with cultural, ecclesial and moral decline, and everything to do with treating people the way Christ did.

CHAPTER 19

How I Got Here

In this chapter, I offer some more backstory.

MY MIND AND heart have changed on the LGBT issue. I am not the only one.[64] But such changes of heart disturb those who do not understand or accept them. I think it would be helpful to offer a bit more backstory into how my mind and heart have changed on this issue—and what hasn't changed.

Christian ethicists teach about all kinds of issues. The basic ethics survey course includes discussion of ethical methodology and a portfolio of issues including political, economic, social, family, bioethical and sexual ethical issues. No one is an expert on all these issues. Especially when constructing lecture notes for the first time, we all begin with what we inherited from our own teachers and mentors. Then we get thrown into the classroom. For me, that happened in 1993, when I first stood before a huge lecture hall of students. I was a terrified 31-year-old rookie.

My dissertation and first publications were about the Holocaust. I had read little in Christian sexual ethics when I first began lecturing about the subject. To the extent that I had a

64 Most recently, Mark Achtemeier, *The Bible's Yes to Same-Sex Marriage: An Evangelical's Change of Heart* (Louisville: Westminster John Knox Press, 2014).

view it was shaped by my parents, my own ardently heterosexual self, my early Baptist experiences as a teenager, my culture shock in dealing with the quite "out" gay culture at Union Seminary in New York, and the conservative views of my early mentor Ron Sider, who is "progressive" on many issues, but not this one.

So I was now a Baptist and evangelical ethics professor. This was my identity and where I worked. I had no freedom and no mental space to consider alternative views on sexuality issues. The fact that I did not have a personal friendship with a gay or lesbian person before I came to Mercer University in 2007 certainly played a role in the near-total ignorance I brought to the subject. My soft Christian heart rejected those who said hateful things about gay people. I knew that was wrong. But I assumed the normative issues were clear, mainly from the creation design theme I discussed earlier. So that was what I said in those few pages in *Kingdom Ethics*, and in class, while working on other issues.

I have lived in Atlanta and gone to church in Decatur for just seven years. But in that time, my life has become enriched by an entirely unexpected influx of LGBT Christians and ex-Christians into my world.

The first major development had nothing to do with Atlanta at all. My beloved baby sister, Katey, a single mother and a Christian, who had been periodically hospitalized with depression and anxiety, including one suicide attempt, came out as a lesbian in 2008. Her testimony is that her depression was largely caused by her inability to even acknowledge her sexuality, let alone integrate it with her faith—and this was largely caused by the Christian teaching she had received.

The fact that traditionalist Christian teaching produces despair in just about every gay or lesbian person who must endure it is surely very relevant information for the LGBT debate. It is certainly shattering news when it comes home to your own family. We end up having real skin in the game.[65]

---

65 Achtemeier, *The Bible's Yes*, ch. 1.

Since Katey's decision to come out, she has been much healthier and happier, though she has struggled to find accepting Christian communities—beyond the Metropolitan Community Churches—in the Virginia towns in which she has lived. I love my sister. Her coming out, and my conservative family's transformative experience of relating to her and now her partner, Karen, have been transformative for me. (Katey not only permitted but also asked me to tell you about her story.)

The goads to my conscience began accelerating. I got a letter around 2009 from a former student telling me of his own struggle with same-sex attraction while in college and how my teaching on this particular issue had contributed to his suffering. He had since come out as gay.

I joined a church that, without any policy decision on the issue, began attracting an influx of gay and lesbian individuals, couples and families. These sisters and brothers became a part of the fabric of our church community.

Some of them made their way into the Sunday school class that I teach each week. For the first time, I was in real-life Christian community with gay Christians. I remember my shock at seeing a strong collection of Rick Warren books in the home of one of these men at a class social. "So, gay Christians also read Rick Warren." These Christians were not liberals. These were Bible Belt evangelicals. And they were also ineradicably gay and lesbian. News flash: Categories upended. Learning happening.

Friendships began to develop. In Christian community, I was experiencing what happens when people begin to know and love each other. Conversations over breakfast. Prayers for one another. Mutual support. Mutual need. Constant learning from the lives of each other.

I do not speak for my congregation, but certainly can say that my heart has changed due in part to what I believe God has been doing among us.

My opinion-writing began reflecting some of these experiences and changing perspectives. I began to read more on the subject. Gay and lesbian Christians, and allies, and others, began seeking me out for conversation.

Mitchell Gold, of Gold and Williams furniture stores, looked me up. He is Jewish and gay. He told me about his then-forthcoming collection of stories by gay people who had grown up in conservative religious households. He told me how his particular deal with God was that God would change Mitchell's sexual orientation by his 21st birthday or Mitchell would kill himself that day. He made it through the day, and eventually committed to improving the lot of kids like himself. Then, he challenged me by name in the conclusion of that book—*Crisis*—to stop being a bystander when it came to the suffering of gay and lesbian people.[66]

He cited my own work *Righteous Gentiles of the Holocaust* against me.[67] That stung. But it was part of the process.

I was teaching at a seminary that is not a flag-waving school, but that has a small number of LGBT students among its diverse constituency. I learned from them, both their strengths and their hurts. I was struck by the brilliance and confidence of our own Cody Sanders, now at Brite Divinity School. I hurt for a gay student friend when I saw him lay hands on an ordinand after he had been denied ordination, only because he was in a covenanted gay relationship.

One day, out of the blue, I heard from Jane Clementi, the mother of Tyler Clementi, the Rutgers student who threw himself off a bridge in New York after being outed and caught on video by his roommate. Her story, and her son's story, affected me deeply. She founded the Tyler Clementi

---

66 Mitchell Gold with Mindy Drucker, *Crisis: 40 Stories Revealing the Personal, Social, and Religious Pain and Trauma of Growing Up Gay in America* (Austin, TX: Greenleaf Book Group Press, 2008), pp. 111-118, 315-318.
67 David P. Gushee, *The Righteous Gentiles of the Holocaust: A Christian Interpretation* (Minneapolis: Augsburg Fortress Press, 1994).

Foundation (http://bit.ly/1127OGf) to help others in her situation. I finally got to meet Jane in October 2014.

I was asked by Cooperative Baptist Fellowship (my denomination) staffer Rick Bennett to help him organize a conversation about these issues for our particular fellowship of churches. I went in unsettled with my older views, but not settled on new ones. After a very careful planning process, we hosted an event at First Baptist in Decatur, Georgia in the spring of 2012. There, something beautiful happened. In a non-coercive and worshipful context we listened to each other. I learned about how many very dear, deeply-hurt-by-the-church-but-still-committed-to-Jesus gay Christians there actually are. They had come from all over the country to be at this event.

In worship and conversation with these brothers and sisters, I felt spiritually renewed. I listened closely to the music and the story of ex-Christian musician Jennifer Knapp (http://bit.ly/1127OGg), rejected by most Christians when she came out as a lesbian, but whom we invited to the conference. I found myself deeply affected as I encountered sisters and brothers who loved Jesus so much that they would not give up on churches that continually hurt them. I also met some ex-churched but not ex-Christian folks who were warily watching to see if the straight Christian types could make church safe for them someday. These meetings made me think in some fresh ways about what it really means to be Church. As Cody Sanders says in his book, "All Christians can learn from LGBTQ lives"—at that 2012 event I learned much.[68]

It began to seem more and more clear to me that Jesus was more likely to be found among these gentle, hurting gay and lesbian Christians than among their adversaries.

I wrote a book manuscript last year. It argued from Scripture that the love of God for all people in Jesus Christ, our human equality in need and gratitude for God's salvation, and

---

68 Cody J. Sanders, *Queer Lessons for the Straight & Narrow: What All Christians Can Learn from LGBTQ Lives* (Macon, GA: Faithlab, 2013).

the fundamental equality of all forgiven sinners in Christian community, at least required clarity about God's love and welcome for gay and lesbian Christians in the Church. Then and there, in loving community together, we could wrestle with the exegetical-biblical-ethical questions I have touched on in earlier chapters.

I exposited the following passages in that book: "for God so loved the world" (John 3:16-17); "no one is good but God alone" (Mark 10:17-18); "a parable to some who trusted in themselves that they were righteous and regarded others with contempt" (Luke 18:9-14); justification by grace through faith for all who believe (Romans 3:21-26); neither Jew nor Greek but one in Christ (Galatians 3:26-28); "love one another with mutual affection" (Romans 12:9-18); "Who are you to pass judgment on servants of another?" (Romans 14:1-4); "don't think of yourself more highly than you ought" (Romans 12:3-8); "he was born blind that God's works might be revealed in him" (John 9:1-5) and several of the texts already discussed here. That manuscript was not quite ready for publication; but it helped prepare me for the work I have done in this one. It certainly showed me that a different way of connecting the biblical dots was quite possible.

My agents pushed me to be more personal in writing that book for what is called a "trade" audience. In the third draft, I realized that my own experience of having been bullied as a young adolescent was profoundly important at the deepest heart level on this issue. I was bullied because I was emotionally sensitive and the sharks on the school bus figured it out. I was bullied because I had terrible skin and that made me an easy target. Many days I wept bitterly at my sense of impotent powerlessness at the hands of my bullies. I realized how much I hated bullying in all its forms. I then connected my own suffering for a condition I could not control to the suffering of others for conditions they cannot control.

It became clear to me that however complex the exegetical and theological issues are, existentially and humanly I needed to wrestle with these questions *in the community of the bullied rather than the community of the bullies.* Better is one day in the company of those bullied by Christians but loved by Jesus than thousands in the company of those wielding scripture to harm the weak and defenseless. I can certainly understand and respect the traditionalist position. But I cannot understand heartless and loveless Christianity. There a clear **no** must be said.

I realized that other than a few pages in *Kingdom Ethics* and *Getting Marriage Right*, the major themes of my writing and teaching career actually all pointed to the same conclusion. *Righteous Gentiles* was about those who stood in solidarity with Jews under Nazi bullying and murder. *Kingdom Ethics* taught about a kingdom of justice, inclusive community, healing, deliverance and love that Jesus lived and died for. *Getting Marriage Right* talked of how much almost everybody wants and needs not just a temporary sexual partner but also a covenanted life partner, which is what Christian marriage is supposed to be. My work on evangelicals and politics, such as *Future of Faith in American Politics*, argued for a constructive justice agenda and not a destructive culture wars agenda.[69] And my *Sacredness of Human Life* book talked about God's immeasurable love and valuing of every human being without exception.

My biblical dot-connecting changed in the way I have slowly outlined in this book. Biblical paradigm plus transformative encounters with real human beings led to a new biblical paradigm, or at least a belief that a new biblical paradigm was plausible—and I knew where my true Christian community for exploring that paradigm was to be found. There was something mysterious and even beautiful about the whole process.

---

69 David P. Gushee, *The Future of Faith in American Politics: The Public Witness of the Evangelical Center.* (Waco, TX: Baylor University Press, 2008).

I hope I have successfully resisted the temptation to attack those who have not made this paradigm leap with me. I acknowledge it is a major leap and that many just won't get there, at least not in my lifetime. Such divergences happen with all paradigm leaps. I do not judge Christ's servants for what they believe Christ is calling them to do. I would hope to be spared their judgment in the same way. Only God is judge.

I also hope to be spared the more merited judgment of those, especially LGBT people themselves, who are rightly way more than tired of being placed under the theological microscope as I've done in this book. It seemed necessary to me to do this in service to that part of the Christian community that might be aided by this kind of reflection. But I will not do it again ... and probably in 50 years people will marvel that books such as this one were ever really needed.

It says something that secular folks, unhindered by centuries of destructive Christian interpretations of the Bible, have so often reached full acceptance of their LGBT neighbors more easily than have Christians.

In large part due to what God has taught me through Deborah, Mike, Tonya, Nick, Mark, Matthew, Sharon, Will, Mitchell, Tyler, Robin, Allison, Chelsea, Harry, Paula, Jennifer, Amy, and Adam; through Katey and Karen, Eve and Cathy, Theron and David, Troy and Brad, Randall and Phillip, Cody and Ben, Jason and Josh, and so many others, my face turns in a new direction. Henceforth my concern related to this issue will mainly be to seek community with those who have suffered the lash of countless Christian rejections. I stand with you. Whatever remains to be resolved, I want to do it alongside you.

I end by apologizing to those who have been hurt by my prior teaching and writing on the LGBT issue. Where I have the chance to amend my written work I will do so. I ask for your forgiveness. I apologize that it has taken me so long to get here. I look forward to continuing the journey together in your company, if you will have me. Meanwhile, I will join you in working for reform in the Christian church, and a safe place for you, your loved ones, and everyone else to follow Jesus.

Ending the Teaching of Contempt

This is the text of the speech I gave at the Reformation Project conference in Washington, D.C., on the evening of November 8, 2014, after the publication of the first edition of Changing Our Mind. The analysis here develops a point noted in passing in one paragraph of chapter 17 of the first edition. It draws heavily on my prior scholarly work, and reflects lessons I was already beginning to learn through disturbing correspondence from LGBT people and those who angrily resist their full acceptance.

I WANT TO talk tonight about a small minority group that was for almost 2000 years the object of a tragically destructive, religiously motivated, contempt on the part of the Church of Jesus Christ.

The Church's teaching about this group was grounded in a number of biblical texts drawn from across the canon of scripture, as they had been interpreted by Christian leaders, and reinforced by centuries of Christian tradition. This destructive pattern of interpreting these texts went back near the origins of Christianity and eventually was very broadly shared by Eastern Orthodox, Roman Catholic, and Protestant strands of Christianity. One could even describe it as a rare point of unity for these warring groups—they could agree on little, but did agree on this. It was hard to find many dissenters to this tradition, as it was grounded in knowledge sources at the very center of Christianity: scripture, tradition, and major church leaders, generation after generation. *Everyone just knew* that the group that was the object of this negative teaching was well worthy of the church's rejection and disdain, that this disdain was "biblical," and that it was attested to by the highest authorities of the Church. Indeed, expressing rejection and disdain for this group became a core part of Christian identity, even Christian piety.

The Church's negative teaching about this group was comprehensive. The Church taught a disdain for this group as a whole and all individuals in it. The Church taught that this group was morally inferior. The Church often taught that this group was evil and had a particular association with Satan. The Church taught that all members of this group would be eternally separated from God. The Church taught that the worship practices of this group were worthless. The Church warned its adherents about associating with this group. The Church ascribed particular vices to this group, including sexual degeneracy and violence, both allegedly aimed especially against children. Even the term used to name this group became a slur, while other even more derogatory slurs were developed.

The Church, at times, was willing to welcome individual members of this group into its fellowship, but this welcome was equivocal. Converts from this group were often relegated to second-class status, if they were welcome at all. Often their group background came up, especially in relation to questions of leadership or ordination. This reflected a lingering taint associated with this group that even conversion could not wash away. Often this half-welcome was withdrawn, and members of this group were exiled not only from the Church, but from the communities in which they lived.

While the leaders of the Church almost never explicitly taught that its members should perpetrate violence on this group, the unfortunate group was indeed regularly victimized by violence. Because these outbreaks of violence were so frequent, a special term was coined to name them, a term which survives to this day. Meanwhile, in everyday life, bullying was common. Name-calling was constant. Social separation was routinely enforced. Preaching regularly communicated contempt for this group. No Christian wanted to be seen as too cozy with this group, for fear of sharing in its moral taint and losing the support of their own family and friends. When this group was targeted by the state, few Christians could be found who would stand is solidarity with them.

From the perspective of the members of this targeted group, Christianity was everywhere, and it was dangerous. The Church's Bible, Cross, tradition, clergy, and scholars carried not positive but negative associations, associations of harm. Members of this targeted group sometimes knew of the beautiful teachings of Christianity. They had heard the great sayings like "love your neighbor as yourself" and "do unto others as you would have them do unto you" and "as you did it to the least of these, you did it to me." But members of this group, very much "the least of these" in Christendom, rarely experienced any Golden Rule, any love, or any mercy, from the Christians who heard and proclaimed these beautiful words.

Have you figured out who I am talking about yet?

Eventually the centuries-old tradition of disdain for this group, which lay deep in the marrow of western civilization and survived the transition into secular modernity, metastasized into a massive eruption of state-sponsored violence. By the time it was over, 1/3 of all members of this group in the entire world had been murdered. I am one of the scholars who have sadly documented that most Christians stood by doing nothing to help the targeted group.

Perhaps you have by now figured out that the targeted group I am talking about is the Jewish people, victims of an unchrist-like body of tradition generally called Christian anti-Judaism, which fed into and married up with a broader economic, cultural, and political anti-Semitism. I discuss this *unchristlike body of Christian tradition* in many of my writings, *including in my first book, Righteous Gentiles of the Holocaust.*

(I will say the word unchristlike 14 times in this address. When you hear it, think: in violation of the nature, ministry, and teaching of Jesus Christ. Or just think: harmful and unloving, the opposite of what Christ was and is like. I chose the term very carefully.)

Anyone looking at the ubiquity of Christian anti-Semitism in, say, 1935, could not have imagined that it would ever change, or would ever get better. Certainly Jews who had been documenting and protesting this tradition for millennia had little reason for hope.

But, amazingly: Within about twenty years of this murderous assault of anti-Semitic state violence during World War II most branches of an appalled Christian world intentionally began changing their teaching about Judaism and the Jewish people.

It was a profound transformation, involving both subtle and overt repudiation of past teaching along with the development of new teaching. And it is very relevant to our gathering tonight.

During the Christian repudiation of two millennia of anti-Judaism and anti-Semitism:

Biblical passages that "everyone" had interpreted a certain way were now interpreted in new ways, or contextualized more seriously, or treated as secondary to more important texts and themes. I will name three pivotal New Testament texts. But there were many other texts whose reading had contributed to Christian anti-Judaism.

Consider the line in *Matthew 27:25* where the crowd crying for Jesus' crucifixion says *"his blood be on us and on our children."* That text used to be taken to mean that that every Jewish person in the world then or later bore responsibility for the death of Jesus. All Jews were viewed as "Christ-killers," and this became a common derogatory term for Jews. Christian kids would call Jewish kids that on the playground. Because of concerted efforts of Christian leaders, eventually in dialogue with Jewish leaders, beginning around 1965, *almost no Christian taught or believed that Jews as a people bore responsibility for the death of Jesus.* Probably none of you have ever heard Jews derided as Christ-killers. And that's a real good change.

John 8:44 reports Jesus saying this to 'the Jews': "*You are from your father the devil, and you choose to do your father's desires. He was a murderer from the beginning and does not stand in the truth, because there is no truth in him. When he lies, he speaks according to his own nature, for he is a liar and the father of lies.*" For centuries in Christendom, that text was taken to mean that Jews as a people were the children of Satan and shared their diabolical father's characteristic behaviors, such as murder and lying. Pious Christian children in Europe used to check their Jewish playmates heads' for the horns that they had been told were hiding under their hair. (True story.) Because of concerted efforts of Christian leaders, eventually in dialogue with Jewish leaders, beginning around 1965, *almost no Christian taught or believed that Jews are the children of Satan.* This passage is now taught very carefully, and it is not taught as applying to "the Jews" as a people. And that's a real good change.

Acts 7 tells the story of the Church's first martyr, Stephen. Have you ever noticed that just before the rocks start flying at his head he says this to his Jewish questioners? "*You stiff-necked people, uncircumcised in heart and ears, you are forever opposing the Holy Spirit, just as your ancestors used to do. Which of the prophets did your ancestors not persecute? They killed those who foretold the coming of the Righteous One, and now you have become his betrayers and murderers. You are the ones that received the law as ordained by angels, and yet you have not kept it.*" For centuries in Christendom, that text was taken to mean that the entire history of the Jewish people has been a story of rebellion against God. This was called the "trail of crimes." Because of concerted efforts of Christian leaders, eventually in dialogue with Jewish leaders, beginning around 1965, *almost no Christian taught or believed the trail of crimes teaching that almost everyone had believed a century earlier.* Leaders now emphasized God's election of the Jewish people, their covenant with God, the grandeur of the Jewish religious tradition, and its continued significance in the world today. And that's a real good change.

And it wasn't just biblical passages that had to be reconsidered.

Historians began digging into the writings of the Church Fathers and other great leaders of the Church. Eventually, the sadly appropriate label "teaching of contempt" came into use to describe the anti-Jewish writings of leaders as diverse as Tertullian, Chrysostom, Hippolytus, Justin Martyr, Eusebius, and Augustine, and many others. Scholars saw that the problem came forward through the Middle Ages and into Protestantism despite the great changes wrought by the Reformation.

Martin Luther, for example, said some of the most hateful things any Christian leader ever said about Jews, including that their synagogues should be burned down, that their religious books should be destroyed, and even that 'we are at fault in not slaying them.' But meanwhile leaders of Eastern Orthodoxy and Roman Catholicism carried forward their own teachings of contempt as well. Christians pondering during the Holocaust whether to rescue Jews found little support in their faith for doing so. Many responded to Jewish distress by invoking anti-Jewish tropes drawn from how the Bible had been interpreted by the Christian tradition and its leaders.

After the war many church bodies eventually abandoned or explicitly repented of this body of traditional post-biblical teaching. For example, the Lutheran churches of both Germany and the U.S. repudiated Luther's terribly damaging writing of 1543 called *On the Jews and Their Lies.* Now, wherever that book is in print, it is accompanied by a warning and very careful contextualization. The Catholic Church also steered sharply away from its former teachings.

These wonderful changes, far too long in coming, have undoubtedly saved Jewish lives all over the world. Certainly Christian understandings of Judaism have been transformed. Anti-Semitism is by no means dead, far from it; indeed, in many places it is disturbingly on the rise, which all Christians must oppose. *But the unchristlike body of Christian teaching tradition that once funded it has been rejected almost everywhere, and certainly in the western world.* Today, at my seminary, the McAfee School of Theology of Mercer University, Jewish rabbis participate in teaching my students about Judaism and the Jewish tradition, and no one thinks twice about it.

And now, 50 years later, probably none of you have ever heard passages like Matthew 27, John 8, and Acts 7 taught in the way they were taught for almost 2000 years. And probably the great majority of you didn't know that there was a centuries-old teaching of contempt by the Church against Jews. You didn't know it because most of you are blissfully young and never had to hear it. You never had to hear it because this *unchristlike body of Christian teaching tradition, rightly labeled a teaching of contempt,* was repudiated 50 years ago. And I hope you never have to encounter it again, after tonight.

∼

I have now been talking about the Church's teaching of contempt against Jews for 2000 words. I have been discussing how the Church finally abandoned this unchristlike body of Christian teaching tradition after 2000 years.

Why in the world would I "go there" in this place tonight?

I am fully aware of the limits of all historical analogies. As a long-time participant in Jewish-Christian dialogue, I am especially aware of the sensitivities of this particular historical analogy. Those tempted to critique the comparison might be interested to know that I have checked it with highly placed

friends in the American Jewish community so as not to mis-
speak, offend, or overreach.

So let me proceed to lay out what I believe to be the appropriate analogies that can be drawn.

I believe that the Church has inflicted a damaging and
ultimately *unchristlike body of Christian tradition, amount-
ing to what can be fairly described as a teaching of contempt,*
against sexual minorities – today called lesbian, gay, bisexual, and transgender persons. This teaching of contempt has
been grounded in what is actually a relatively small number
of biblical texts, as they have been interpreted by Christian
leaders, and reinforced by centuries of Christian tradition. It
has been hard to find many dissenters to this tradition, as it
has been grounded in knowledge sources at the very center of
Christianity: scripture, tradition, and the leaders of the church,
generation after generation. Everyone just knew that gay, lesbian, bisexual, and transgender people were well worthy of the
church's rejection and disdain—not just in their sexual desires
or practices, but in their persons. For some Christians, even
today, being anti-gay became woven into the heart of Christian identity and even piety.

The church's anti-gay teaching was comprehensive. The
Church taught a disdain for LGBT people as a whole and all
individuals in the group. The Church taught that LGBT people
are morally inferior. The Church sometimes taught that LGBT
people are evil. Certainly it taught and sometimes still teaches
that LGBT people are by definition excluded from heaven. The
Church warned its adherents about associating with LGBT
people. The Church at various times ascribed particular vices
to LGBT people, including sexual degeneracy, especially
against children.

The Church at times was willing to welcome individual
LGBT people into its fellowship, but this welcome was equivocal. LGBT people were often relegated to second-class status,
surfacing especially in relation to questions of leadership in
the church. And often this half-welcome was withdrawn. (One

Jewish reader of this lecture commented to me that in this sense it was easier in most eras of Christianity for Jews to find full and unequivocal welcome in the Church than it has ever been for gay and lesbian people to find such welcome. Conversion meant a Jew became a Christian, but conversion doesn't meant a gay person becomes a straight person. Not that people haven't tried.)

While the leaders of the Church almost never explicitly taught that its members should perpetrate violence on LGBT people, they were and sometimes still are victimized by outbreaks of violence. Schoolyard bullying was common. Name-calling was constant. Social separation was routinely enforced. Preaching regularly communicated disdain for LGBT people. Few Christians wanted to be seen as too cozy with LGBT people, for fear of sharing in their moral taint and losing the support of their own family and friends. The very words used to describe LGBT people functioned as slurs. When LGBT people were excluded or targeted by the state, few Christians could be found who would stand up for LGBT people.

From the perspective of LGBT people, Christianity has been both ubiquitous and dangerous. The Church's Bible, Cross, tradition, clergy, and scholars, have carried negative associations, associations of harm. LGBT people, millions of them raised in the Church and deeply committed to Jesus, have known of the beautiful teachings of Christianity. They have heard the great sayings like "love your neighbor as yourself" and "do unto others as you would have them do unto you" and "as you did it to the least of these, you did it to me." But LGBT people, very much the least of these in Christendom, rarely experienced toward themselves, if they were out as LGBT, any Golden Rule, any love, and mercy, from the Christians who heard and proclaimed these beautiful words.

So now I have made my historical analogy. But immediately I again acknowledge that analogies have their limits.

I am not claiming that LGBT people have faced genocide.

But it is true that it remains physically dangerous to be an LGBT person in many places. I have students from other parts of the world who tell me of routine violence inflicted against sexual minorities in their home countries. We have heard of such violence already this evening.

There has been no genocide—though there has been persecution and murder, including on a large scale in Nazi Germany.

Still, we speak of a group of people that even today, even in our country, sometimes hear diatribes, with quotes from scripture, suggesting that they should all be executed by the state. I once was the next guest on a Christian radio show where a preacher had just said that.

The analogy breaks down in an interestingly different way.

A Jewish child discovering the contempt of the wider Christian world could at least go home and find support there. But a gay child discovering the contempt of the wider Christian world has often faced a devastating lack of support at home as well. I will say more about that in a moment.

And here is one more way the analogy breaks down, but this time more constructively:

The *unchristlike teaching of contempt for Jews has been discredited*. No mainstream Christian leader that I know of teaches it anymore, at least not here in this country. The Bible didn't change. What the Bible was understood to mean changed a great deal.

The unchristlike teaching of contempt for LGBT people is, in my view, *in the process of being discredited, of breaking down*, even as we speak. *Every year elements of it lose ground.* I am now confident that Christianity is undergoing the same repudiation of an unchristlike body of tradition today, in regard to LGBT people, as happened 50 years ago in regard to anti-Semitism.

So this is the point of my comparison—I am comparing two different unchristlike bodies of Christian teaching tradition, one of which has been discredited and abandoned, the

other of which needs to be and is in the process of being discredited and abandoned. We must celebrate the progress being
made in repudiating the teaching of contempt against that
1/20th of the human family who are LGBT. And we must fin-
ish the job as soon as we can.

There has been progress. But still, all is not well. Teaching
and behavior that harms our own sexual minorities has not
disappeared, not by a long shot. LGBT people are still not
treated as equals, as kin, in the family of faith. They are often
rejected by their families, churches, schools, and friends. Their
gifts continue to be blocked. In just two weeks since my own
announcement of standing in solidarity with LGBT Christians,
I have heard from literally scores of young people, parents,
and others with their harrowing tales of rejection and harm.
Brothers and sisters, this must not continue.

∾

*Increasingly, my focus moves to the continued suffering of
LGBT young people. Their plight is important.*

Consider this: The Center for American Progress here in
Washington did a key policy report on LGBT homeless youth.
(http://ampr.gs/1GwkDM1)

"Homeless youth" are "*unaccompanied young people between
the ages of 12 and 24 for whom it is not possible to safely live
with a relative or in another safe alternative living arrangement.*"
Among these homeless youth are those who have left home
willingly and without their family's knowledge—"runaway"
youth—and those who have left home against their will, at the
hands of their guardians—"throwaway" youth.

CAP cites commonly reported estimates that there are
between 2.4 million and 3.7 million homeless youth between
the ages of 12-24.

*LGBT youth are vastly overrepresented among the home-
less youth population.* "Several state and local studies from
across the United States have found shockingly disproportionate rates of homelessness among LGBT youth compared to

non-LGBT youth. Estimates of homeless youth ... suggest that between 9 percent and 45 percent of these youth are LGBT.

The study parameters differ a bit in terms of age, but here are the percentage of homeless youth in some specific locations who identify as LGBT, with all studies undertaken since 2000:

NYC: 33%
Seattle: 39%
Los Angeles: 25%
Illinois: 15%
Chicago: 22%

It is not hard to figure out why LGBT kids constitute such a high percentage of homeless youth. The most common reasons that LGBT homeless youth cite for being out of their homes are family rejection and conflict. And much family rejection is religiously motivated. It is based on this very same unchristlike body of Christian teaching I have been talking about. It destroys lives and fractures families. In the name of faithfulness to scripture, which is so very, very tragic.

Caitlin Ryan, who directs the Family Acceptance Project (http://bit.ly/1127OpR) at SFSU, spoke to me last week. She described a tragic vortex. More and more children and youth are coming out as LGBT at younger ages. FAP has found that the average age of coming out is now a little over age 13. And increasingly in her research and family support work, she reports that children are identifying as gay at much younger ages - between ages seven and 12.

Because they are younger, these kids have fewer coping skills and options for finding support outside the home, so their self-identity and sense of self-worth are even more vulnerable than they would be if they were older. Thus, when their families learn that their children are LGBT, if those families reject them it comes as an even more crushing and debilitating blow to the sense that they are good and valuable people. This affects their ability to love and care for themselves, to avoid dangerous and high-risk behaviors, to have hope, and to plan for the future.

The data is clear that all too often when young people come out or are found to be LGBT, they are met with family rejection, which can include violent responses.

FAP has identified and researched dozens of different family responses to their LGBT child and measured them to show the relationship between experiencing specific family-accepting and family-rejecting behaviors during adolescence with their health and well-being as young adults.

The higher the level of family rejection, the higher the likelihood of negative health, mental health, and behavioral problems. The higher the level of family acceptance, the more that LGBT youth are protected against risk and the greater their sense of self-worth, overall health and well-being.

Some of the family rejecting behaviors documented and studied by FAP include hitting/slapping/physical harming, verbal harassment and name-calling, exclusion from family activities, blocking access to LGBT friends, events, and resources, blaming the child when he/she experiences abuse or discrimination, pressuring the child to be more masculine or feminine, threatening God's punishment, making the child pray and attend religious services to change their LGBT identity, sending them for reparative therapy, declaring that the child brings shame to the family, and not talking about their LGBT identity or making them keep it a secret from family members and others.

FAP found a direct correlation between "highly rejecting" families and the following:

- more than eight times as likely to have attempted suicide at least once
- more than six times as likely to report high levels of depression
- more than three times as likely to use illegal drugs

- more than three times as likely to be high-risk for HIV and STDs

FAP found that even being a little less rejecting and a little more accepting reduces the likelihood of these harmful behaviors substantially. For example: LGBT youth from "moderately rejecting" families were only twice as likely to attempt suicide compared to LGBT peers from non-rejecting families.

~

I received this text from the program director for the Family Acceptance Project. She said: "I hear stories every day that are heartrending, children sleeping in snow banks because there are no youth shelters. Last January I had five children kicked out of religious homes, with literally nowhere to go. One girl slept in the snow in front of her school. She was 16."

Runaway or kicked-out LGBT youth who end up on the streets as homeless youth are more likely to be homeless for longer periods than their peers, according to the CAP report data. The problem appears to be especially severe for transgender youth.

Not much good comes of homelessness, and that is certainly true for homeless LGBT youth. The CAP report documents all kinds of problems:

- much more likely to end in child welfare or institutional care systems after being removed from home due to conflict over LGBT-related issues;
- leaving home because of family rejection is the greatest predictor of ending up in the juvenile justice system for LGBT youth;
- placements in foster care or other housing all too often end in further homelessness because of bias against LGBTs or abuse and mistreatment;
- once in the justice system, LGBT youth and young adults are at increased risk of being labeled sex offenders even when not convicted of sex-related crimes;

- disproportionate difficulty for LGBT youth in accessing safe shelter while homeless;
- disproportionately likely to engage in 'survival sex' to meet expenses, increasing vulnerability to rape, disease, violence;
- disproportionately high rates of victimization by robbery, assault, rape, and hate crimes while on streets;
- disproportionately bad health outcomes including drug and alcohol abuse;
- disproportionate suicidal ideation and attempts.

This has to stop. And the only way—or at least a major way--to make it stop is to bring an end to the *unchristlike Christian teaching* about LGBT people as once occurred in that body of unchristlike Christian teaching about Jews. We do in fact need a reformation.

∽

I suggest that there are some lessons to be learned from how the Christian teaching of contempt against Jews ended, lessons relevant to ending this unchristlike teaching of con-tempt against our sexual minorities, 1/20th of the human and Christian population.

We must highlight the human costs—which involves attend-ing to the real human beings affected. Engage people's hearts, not just their minds, with the real human beings who suffer under this teaching. No conversation about 'the LGBT issue' should any longer take place without hearing the voice of LGBT people themselves.

We must call people on it when they slip back into the old derogations and slurs, especially religious leaders—which involves identifying what the current minimal decent standard now looks like, then guarding that line as we move for more progress. We must not let people slip backwards without being challenged.

We must engage the destructively-cited biblical texts in the ways done by reformers of Christian anti-Judaism since the 1960s—which involves fresh research on the background and meaning of the texts, broader contextualization of the circumstances in which they were written, and constructive reinterpretation in the Spirit of Christ. Many important recent works are doing this.

But one major lesson I draw from the struggle related to Christian anti-Judaism is that it is best not to get too fixated on the six or seven big passages most commonly cited in the anti-gay teaching tradition. Because when change happened on Christian anti-Judaism, it wasn't just about altering the reading of those texts, but *changing the conversation to the more central themes and texts related to following the way of Jesus.* Thus:

We must change the conversation to what it means to live in the way Jesus taught us.

I noticed this in studying Christian rescuers of Jews during the Holocaust. This righteous minority of Christians who rescued Jews, right in the teeth of unchristlike anti-Jewish Christian traditions, cited motivating texts like the Golden Rule, the Double Love Command, the Good Samaritan, and the saying about being our brother's keepers. They highlighted broader biblical themes like the sacred worth of every person, and our obligation as Christians to be compassionate, merciful, and just. Somehow John 8 or Acts 7 or Matthew 27 just fell away, or were read differently, in light of these towering biblical texts and moral convictions. I now believe that when we spend all our time arguing about texts like Leviticus 18 and 1 Corinthians 6 and Romans 1 we miss the opportunity to call Christians back to the texts and themes that are and should be more central in their everyday Christian lives.

Then, when challenged,

We must cling to Jesus' example and the way he conducted his ministry. We must spend a lot of time in the gospels. If we do we might notice his warnings about religious self-righteousness

and contempt for others deemed to be sinners; his embrace
of outcasts and marginalized people; his attacks on those
religious leader types who block access to God's grace; his
elevating as examples those who simply and humbly pray for
God's mercy; his teachings about God's prodigious grace; and
perhaps above all his death on the cross for the sins of all of us,
beginning with each of us as "chief of sinners." We must focus
tightly on Jesus Christ, our Savior and Lord.

We must listen for and be ready for the Spirit of God—
which looks like our hard hearts melting, our calcified minds
changing, our spirits repenting; it looks like our churches
growing more inclusive, our courage deepening, and our love
for unwanted strangers growing fierce. It looks like joyful
cross-bearing for Jesus' sake. It looks like solidarity with the
oppressed. It looks like strangely abundant joy.

This work is hard, because:

- *There is the issue itself, with all its complexity, but then there's
  also the authority problem in the Church, and the difficulty
  of admitting we were wrong.* So it's never just about a few
  Bible passages and how they should be interpreted. It's
  about capital A Authority—of scripture, tradition, and
  contemporary church leaders, and who gets to say who
  has got it right. It's also about the general unwillingness
  of Christians to admit that they might have gotten
  something wrong, either individually or collectively. That
  idea is very unsettling, and it's hard to face, and those
  responsible for institutions especially struggle with
  admitting prior error. But admitting prior error is called
  repentance, a concept we should be familiar with. And
  the Church has repented before. It's really important to
  remind people that the church has gotten some key things
  wrong before, has repented, and has recovered to enter
  a more faithful path of discipleship. We did it on slavery,
  race, and anti-Semitism. We can do it now.

- *Breaking open a settled paradigm seems to take transformative encounters with God and people, empowered by the Holy Spirit.* But not everyone has such encounters or is open to them. One reason we need to come out as LGBT or allies is so we can make such transformative encounters available to more of those who have not had them. Everyone who comes out makes it harder for evangelical America to believe that this is someone else's issue. Meanwhile, it's hard for Christians to change their minds if they never have an encounter with an LGBT person or a fiercely committed ally.

- *People have woven the LGBT narrative into the broader cultural decline narrative,* to which many Christians are viscerally committed. Here, once again, LGBT people turn into symbols. So bringing an end to the marginalization and mistreatment of LGBT Christians requires helping people to see that they are not agents of cultural decline, but marginalized brothers and sisters in Christ who just want full inclusion in the community of faith.

Ultimately, gay, lesbian, bisexual, and transgender Christians must be accepted and welcomed in the Church on the same basis as any other sinner saved by grace. Their – your – partic- ipation in Christian community must be governed by the same principles that apply to any other believer.

For many in this room such a claim is an obvious truth. But as you well know it is not a truth universally acknowledged. In the end, incremental progress toward partial, conditional half-acceptance is not enough. You (we) are right to ask and to require full, unequivocal, equal acceptance in Christ's church on the same terms as every other sinner saved by the grace of God in Jesus Christ.

This includes the fierce debate over sexual ethics as it applies to LGBT people.

If LGBT participation in Christian community were gov- erned by the same principles that apply to all other believers,

believers of every tribe, tongue, race, and nation, that would settle the sexual ethics debate, once and for all.

What is the sexual ethics standard that applies to followers of Christ? *Celibacy outside of lifetime covenantal marriage, monogamous fidelity within lifetime covenantal marriage.* That norm, as I argue in my book, applies to all Christians. It is demanding, countercultural, and essential to the well-being of adults and children.

I now see that this same covenantal-marital norm should apply to that particular minority, 1/20th of the human and Christian population, whose difference from the majority relates to sexual orientation and gender identity. They too should be held to the same standard as every other Christian. Celibacy outside lifetime covenantal marriage, monogamous fidelity within lifetime covenantal marriage.

The opponents of this gathering think that what you are about is moral chaos and the weakening of Christian morality. I think what you are about is inclusion of the LGBT minority of the church into the same rigorous Christian morality that applies to any other believer. That is certainly my agenda. And I truly apologize that it took me twenty years to figure out this very simple truth and get on board.

Let me close by saying I applaud you. Matthew Vines and friends, you impress and inspire me. You are a youth-led movement in the Church demanding a better future for the whole Church. You are a movement for the liberation of the oppressed, like many of the most important movements for human dignity in history. You are a movement of high energy and distinctively evangelical hopefulness based on the power of God to advance God's kingdom. You are a movement whose time has come.

I will henceforth oppose any form of discrimination against you. I will *seek to stand in solidarity with you who have suffered the lash of countless Christian rejections.* I will be your ally in every way I know how to be.

I will view what got us here as one of those tragic situations in Church history in which well-intentioned Christians, just trying to follow Jesus – including myself, for a long time -- misread sacred scripture and caused great harm to oppressed people, in what turned out to be a violation of the character, teaching, and example of Jesus Christ. It has happened before, we have repented before, and we have changed before. We can do it again. I believe it will happen, sooner than many think. This debate will be over and many will wonder what the fuss was about …

Together, one day, all of us will dine together at the banquet table of the Son of God. We will be asked whether we loved and served Jesus with everything that was in us. And then together we will have a really great party. This room is a foretaste of the future of the church. And the church is a foretaste of that kingdom banquet. Remember this text (Rev. 21:3-4)?

"See, the home of God is among mortals.

He will dwell with them;

they will be his peoples,

and God himself will be with them,

he will wipe every tear from their eyes.

Death will be no more;

mourning and crying and pain will be no more,

for the first things have passed away."

And we shall all be one, at last. God bless you, brothers and sisters.

View the video of David Gushee's historic
speech at: http://bit.ly/1GwkE2k

References

Achtemeier, Mark. *The Bible's Yes to Same-Sex Marriage: An Evangelical's Change of Heart.* Louisville: Westminster John Knox Press, 2014.

Barton, Bernadette. *Pray the Gay Away: The Extraordinary Lives of Bible Belt Gays.* New York/London: New York University Press, 2012.

Bird, Phyllis A. "The Bible in Christian Ethical Deliberation Concerning Homosexuality: Old Testament Contributions," in *Homosexuality, Science, and the "Plain Sense" of Scripture*, ed. David L. Balch. Grand Rapids, MI: William B. Eerdmans Publishing Company, 2000.

Bonhoeffer, Dietrich. *Ethics: Dietrich Bonhoeffer Works, Volume 6.* Minneapolis: Fortress Press Press, 2005.

Brownson, James V. *Bible, Gender, Sexuality: Reframing the Church's Debate on Same-Sex Relationships.* Grand Rapids: William B. Eerdmans Publishing Company, 2013.

Brueggemann, Walter. *Genesis: Interpretation: Bible Commentary for Teaching and Preaching.* Atlanta: John Knox Press, 1982.

Cahill, Lisa Sowle. *Between the Sexes: Foundations for a Christian Ethics of Sexuality.* Philadelphia: Fortress Press Press/New York: Paulist Press, 1985.

Chu, Jeff. *Does Jesus Really Love Me? A Gay Christian's Pilgrimage in Search of God in America.* New York: HarperCollins, 2013.

Douglas, Mary. *Purity and Danger: An Analysis of Concepts of Pollution and Taboo*. London: Routledge Classics, 2002.

Farley, Margaret. *Just Love: A Framework for Christian Sexual Ethics*. New York/London: Continuum, 2006.

Friedman, Richard Elliott and Shawna Dolansky. *The Bible Now*. Oxford: Oxford University Press, 2011.

Gagnon, Robert A.J. *The Bible and Homosexual Practice: Texts and Hermeneutics*. Nashville: Abingdon Press, 2001.

Gold, Mitchell with Mindy Drucker. *Crisis: 40 Stories Revealing the Personal, Social, and Religious Pain and Trauma of Growing Up Gay in America*. Austin, TX: Greenleaf Book Group Press, 2008.

Greenberg, Irving. *For the Sake of Heaven and Earth: The New Encounter Between Judaism and Christianity*. Philadelphia: Jewish Publication Society, 2004.

Grimsrud, Ted and Mark Thiessen Nation, *Reasoning Together: A Conversation on Homosexuality*. Scottdale, PA: Herald Press, 2008.

Gushee, David P. *The Future of Faith in American Politics: The Public Witness of the Evangelical Center*. Waco, TX: Baylor, 2008.

Gushee, David P. *Getting Marriage Right: Realistic Counsel for Saving and Strengthening Marriages*. Grand Rapids: Baker, 2004.

Gushee, David P. *The Righteous Gentiles of the Holocaust: A Christian Interpretation*. Minneapolis: Augsburg Fortress Press, 1994

Gushee, David P. *The Sacredness of Life: Why an Ancient Biblical Vision is Key to the World's Future*. Grand

Rapids, MI: William B. Eerdmans Publishing Company, 2013.

Gushee, David P., and Isaac B. Sharp, editors. *Evangelical Social Ethics: Converting America and Its Christians, 1944-2014* (Library of Theological Ethics). Louisville: Westminster John Knox Press, forthcoming 2015.

Hays, Richard B. *First Corinthians: Interpretation Bible Commentary.* Louisville: John Knox Press, 1997.

Hill, Wesley. *Washed and Waiting: Reflections on Christian Faithfulness and Homosexuality.* Grand Rapids: Zondervan, 2010.

Jordan, Mark D. *The Invention of Sodomy in Christian Theology.* Chicago: University of Chicago Press, 1997.

Lee, Justin. *Torn: Rescuing the Gospel from the Gays-vs.-Christians Debate.* New York: Jericho Books, 2012.

Loader, William. *The New Testament on Sexuality.* Grand Rapids: William B. Eerdmans Publishing Company, 2012.

Marin, Andrew. *Love is an Orientation: Elevating the Conversation with the Gay Community.* Downers Grove, IL: Intervarsity Press, 2009.

Marks, Jeremy. *Exchanging the Truth of God for a Lie: One Man's Spiritual Journey to Find the Truth about Homosexuality and Same-Sex Partnerships,* 2nd edition. Glasgow: Bell & Bain, 2009.

Martin, Dale B. *Sex and the Single Savior: Gender and Sexuality in Biblical Interpretation.* Louisville: Westminster John Knox, 2006.

Milgrom, Jacob. *Leviticus: A Continental Commentary.* Minneapolis: Fortress Press Press, 2004.

Myers, David G. *Psychology*, 10th edition. New York: Worth
    Publishers, 2013.

Noth, Martin. *Leviticus: Old Testament Library*. Philadelphia:
    Westminster Press, 1965.

Paris, Jenell Williams. *The End of Sexual Identity: Why Sex Is
    Too Important to Define Who We Are*. Downers Grove,
    IL: Intervarsity Press, 2011.

Piper, John and Wayne Grudem, *Recovering Biblical Manhood
    and Womanhood: A Response to Evangelical Feminism*.
    Wheaton, IL: Crossway Books, 2012).

Roberts, Christopher Chennault. *Creation and Covenant: The
    Significance of Sexual Difference in the Moral Theology of
    Marriage*. New York/London, T & T Clark, 2007.

Rogers, Jack. *Jesus, the Bible, and Homosexuality: Explode the
    Myths, Heal the Church*. Louisville: Westminster John
    Knox, 2006.

Ruether, Rosemary. *Faith and Fratricide: The Theological
    Roots of Anti-Semitism*. Minneapolis: Winston Press,
    1974.

Sanders, Cody J. *Queer Lessons for the Straight & Narrow:
    What All Christians Can Learn from LGBTQ Lives*.
    Macon, GA: Faithlab, 2013.

Ruden, Sarah. *Paul Among the People: The Apostle
    Reinterpreted and Reimagined in His Own Time*. New
    York: Image Books, 2010.

Stassen, Glen H. and David P. Gushee, *Kingdom Ethics:
    Following Jesus in Contemporary Context*. Downers
    Grove, IL: Intervarsity Press, 2003.

Stowe, Harriet Beecher. *Uncle Tom's Cabin*. New York: Barnes
    & Noble Classics, [1852] 2003.

Thiselton, Anthony C. *The First Epistle to the Corinthians: New International Greek Testament Commentary.* Grand Rapids, MI/Cambridge: William B. Eerdmans Publishing Company, 2000.

Trible, Phyllis. *Texts of Terror: Literary-Feminist Readings of Biblical Narratives.* Philadelphia: Fortress Press Press, 1984.

VanderWal-Gritter, Wendy. *Generous Spaciousness: Responding to Gay Christians in the Church.* Grand Rapids: Brazos, 2014.

Vasey, Michael. *Strangers and Friends: A New Exploration of Homosexuality and the Bible.* London: Hodder & Stoughton, 1995.

Vines, Matthew. *God and the Gay Christian: The Biblical Case in Support of Same-Sex Relationships.* New York: Convergent Books, 2014.

von Rad, Gerhard. Genesis: *Old Testament Library,* revised edition. Philadelphia: Westminster Press, 1972.

Webb, William J. *Slaves, Women & Homosexuals: Exploring the Hermeneutics of Cultural Analysis.* Downers Grove, IL: Intervarsity Press, 2001.

Wenham, Gordon J. *Leviticus: New International Commentary on the Old Testament.* Grand Rapids: William B. Eerdmans Publishing Company, 1979.

Wilson, Ken. *A Letter to my Congregation: An evangelical pastor's path to embracing people who are gay, lesbian and transgender into the company of Jesus.* Canton, MI: Read the Spirit Books, 2014.

Wold, Donald J. *Out of Order: Homosexuality in the Bible and the Ancient Near East.* Grand Rapids: Baker, 1998.

If you enjoyed this book, you may also enjoy

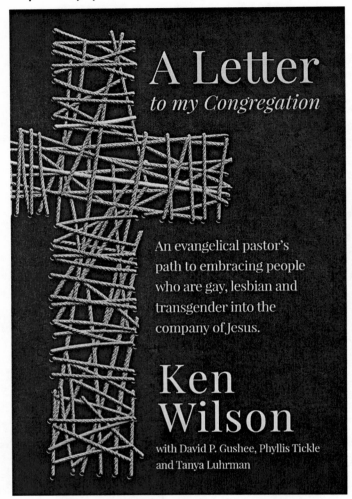

A Letter
to my Congregation

An evangelical pastor's
path to embracing people
who are gay, lesbian and
transgender into the
company of Jesus.

Ken
Wilson

with David P. Gushee, Phyllis Tickle
and Tanya Luhrman

"A breakthrough work coming from the heart of evangelical Christianity,"
writes theologian David Gushee. "Wilson shows how God has led him
on a journey toward a rethinking of what the fully authoritative and
inspired Bible ought to be taken to mean in the life of the church today."

www.ALetterToMyCongregation.com

ISBN: 978-1-939880-30-47

4, 5, 9, 13, 16, 17-18, 25, 22, 51,52, Chapt. 10,

102-3, 108, 115, 116

A child, if Touched "inappropriately" by an adult, or other knows IT is _wrong_. To attempt To say that same sex sex is okay is _wrong._

CPSIA information can be obtained at www.ICGtesting.com
Printed in the USA
LVOW12s2336220415

435735LV00004B/290/P

9 781939 880932